Sorry, I Have to Take

A Story About Breaking Free from Digital Distractions

- David B. Rust & Bradley J. Kramer -

Copyright © 2013, David B. Rust & Bradley J. Kramer.
All rights reserved under all copyright conventions.

ISBN-13: 978-1494759667

ISBN-10: 1494759667

Printed in the United States of America

No part of this publication may be reproduced, stored in a retrieval system, or transmitted in any form or by means, electronic, mechanical photocopying, recording, scanning, or otherwise, except as permitted under Section 107 or 108 of the 1976 United States Copyright Act, without either prior written permission of the publisher, or authorization through payment or the appropriate per-copy fee to the Copyright Clearance Center, Inc. The scanning, uploading and distribution of this book via the Internet or via any other means without the permission of the publisher is illegal and punishable by law. Please purchase only authorized electronic editions, and do not participate or encourage electronic piracy of copyrighted materials. Your support of the author's rights is appreciated.

This is a work of fiction. Names, characters, places and incidents either are products of the author's imagination or are used fictitiously. Any resemblance to actual events or locales or persons, living or dead, is entirely coincidental.

To Tanja and Nancy, for everything you have taught us about focus, concentration, and especially authenticity.

Preface

If you are like many of my business clients, you have renamed the "Information Age" the "Too Much Information Age." Deluged, as you are, by a never-ending stream of e-mails, tweets, texts, social media posts, and mobile phone calls that can come at any time, you feel absolutely awash in information—often trivial, sometimes important, occasionally vital, but always urgent, insistently demanding that you drop everything you are, and deal with it now. As a result, you are pulled from issue to issue, often without actually addressing the issue properly or fitting your actions into a strategic, long-term plan. You feel tossed about, out of control, almost helpless within a constantly churning whirlpool of electronic activity, and you feel yourself going down quickly. Your work suffers, your attitude suffers, your health suffers, and your relationships with your family, friends, and coworkers suffer. There has to be a way out of this, you think; there has to be a solution. The only problem is, you cannot seem to find it.

If this describes you and if you are looking for a way to control this chaos and move forward at a reasonable, productive pace, this book is for you. In this book, I have distilled years of experience helping business professionals to understand three seemingly simple principles—Focus, Concentration, and Authenticity. With Brad Kramer's help, I have explored these principles within a story of a sales vice president who similarly struggles with information overload. In addition, I follow this story with a brief summary of these principles as well as several practical tips as to how you can implement them and keep track of your progress.

My hope is that you will learn from *Sorry, I Have to Take This*, implement the principles, and enjoy stronger relationships with your family members, coworkers, and friends. —David B. Rust

Visit www.sorryihavetotakethis.com to access additional resources associated with this book.

Contents

PART ONE: BEN'S JOB 1

Home 3
Driving to Work 9
Miamiville 15
Phil 23
The Big Meeting 31
Ben's Surprise 41
After the Meeting 49
Late Again 57
Driving Home 65
The Next Day 75
At the Soccer Field 85
Billy's Garage 91
Billy 99
Back at the Office 107
Bobbi's Advice 115
Sarah's Response 123
Pittsburgh 131
More Interviews 141
Zephyr Corp. 147
I-71 155
The Fleischmann Estate 165
The Caretaker 175
Phil Again 185
Miamiville Again 191
Sarah's Suggestions 197
Preliminaries 207

Another Big Meeting 213
Conclusion 219
Epilogue 229
PART TWO: BEN'S PRINCIPLES 231
Principle 1: Focus 233
   Explanation of the problem 234
   Self-evaluation 236
   Solutions 237
Principle 2: Concentration 245
   Explanation of the problem 246
   Self-evaluation 246
   Solutions 247
Principle 3: Authenticity 251
   Explanation of the problem 252
   Self-evaluation 254
   Solutions 254
Acknowledgements 259
About the Authors 261

Part One: Ben's Job

Sorry, I Have to Take This

Home

Many business professionals live with a degree of chaos and have little time for serious thinking. One of the symptoms of people in this situation is that they lack focus. They frequently let their attention vacillate unsuccessfully between their personal and professional lives.

By many accounts, Ben should have felt pretty good about himself and his situation. He had a wonderful wife—his college sweetheart, Sarah—two great kids—Aaron, eight, and Amy, ten—a spacious house in Loveland, Ohio, USA—a two-story brick colonial with a three-car garage in an exclusive development—and a job he had drooled over for years—regional vice president of sales for DigitALL, a company specializing in setting up and servicing computers and networks on a 24/7 basis within corporations. The problem was, Ben didn't know what he was feeling. He didn't have time.

"Sarah, have you seen my cell phone?" Ben bellowed, more or less in his wife's direction.

"It's on the table," came the distant reply. Ben turned and stared blankly at the display table in the hallway. As far as he knew it was the only table in the house that was not piled high with stuff. Nothing was there, just family photos and a terra cotta vase his wife had made in high school. Ben picked up the vase, just to make sure nothing was behind it and scratched himself on its crudely repaired handle.

"Which one?" he asked, sucking on his hurt finger.

"Which what?"

"Which table?"

"The one in our bedroom."

Ben ran up the stairs, skipping every other step, and bounded into the master bedroom. He scanned the two end tables flanking their bed. Half-emptied glasses, partially read books, old *Tennis* magazines, and bills cluttered them like fallen leaves. He pushed aside a still wet towel, accidentally knocking the TV remote into a medicine bottle and spilling its contents onto the floor. Orange pills suddenly dotted their dark blue carpet like a constellation of dying stars. Again, nothing.

"Which one in our bedroom?" he yelled over his shoulder into the bathroom.

Ben felt a shove from behind as Sarah, all elbows as she finished fixing her ever-present ponytail, wriggled by him, bumping him in the head. "Honestly, I don't know how you survive in the business world. You can't find anything."

Reaching deftly beside the computer, to the left of the modem, behind the speakers, Sarah magically produced the missing cell phone.

"Is this what you were looking for?" she asked, suddenly playful, holding the device between her index finger and thumb like a doggie treat for their pet Schnauzer.

"Thanks, I must have put it there while I was scanning the computer. I still can't figure out how we got a virus. Not with all the security programs we have running on that thing. I even installed a second firewall just in case." Ben continued complaining about the computer and grabbed absently for the phone, but Sarah, smiling broadly, pulled it away.

"No, no, no. You have to pay my finder's fee first." She then leaned forward and stuck out her lips in anticipation of a kiss, or more.

Ben's surge of gratitude upon seeing his Smartphone again now turned to panic. He grabbed for the phone, but Sarah, twisting to the side, eluded him.

"Come on, Sarah, we don't have time for this."

"Sure, we do, lover," Sarah said softly, still holding the phone at arm's length away from Ben. Ben had never noticed how long her arms were before, and seemingly double-jointed. He lunged again. Sarah twisting away, laughing, grabbed him from behind with her free hand, pulling him close—the cell phone still out of his reach.

"The kids are eating their breakfast downstairs," she whispered. "How about we have a 'snack' too?"

Sarah sucked Ben's earlobe seductively, but Ben was having none of it. He gripped the hand that entrapped him and slowly, deliberately pulled it away from him. Still holding Sarah's wrist, Ben stood upright, turned, and faced her.

"Sarah, be serious. I have to get ready for my big meeting. I have seven thousand things to do. I can't. I don't have time for this."

Sarah, her smile gone now, twisted out of his grasp and turned away from him. Her robe, once loose, was now pulled tightly around her. "That's the problem, isn't it, Ben? There's never any time. No time for us. No time for the kids. No time for anything but work, work, work, work. Sometimes I wish you had never taken that new job."

"Come on, Sarah," he protested, rubbing his scratched hand, still eyeing the cell phone. "That's not fair. We've talked about this. We will have time, just not now. Once I get this new job under control, things will be better. I promise. You'll see. I just have to get over this hump."

Ben approached her and held her by her shoulders. Sarah did not respond. She just stood there, looking out the window. Ben could almost hear the clock ticking. He had to get going, but he needed his cell phone and could not think of a way of getting it without upsetting Sarah further. Finally Sarah said something.

"Do you see that old car the Fergussons have?"

"Yeah," Ben said, rubbing her shoulders, hoping that that would help her hurry. It was already 7:38, according to the clock in the corner.

"The dark blue one with the white roof in the driveway?"

"Uh-huh." Of course, Ben knew the car. It was a Mustang convertible—a classic V-6 from the 60s. He had even offered to buy it once, but Scott Fergusson was not ready to part with it. Nonetheless, Ben looked out the window. From his angle the Mustang looked distorted, elongated somehow by the glass.

"My parents had a car like that once when I was growing up, and my sister and I used to fight for the privilege of driving it. And most of the time, my parents let us, allowing us to take it to school or to see friends—except for Wednesday nights. That was their night to use it. It was their 'date night.'"

Inwardly Ben groaned. Not the "date night" thing again. He knew what was coming. He'd heard it so many times before he practically had Sarah's spiel memorized and could mouth the most salient points with her—how her parents would not always go on elaborate dates, how they would sometimes just drive to the mall and walk around together, how they once went to a grocery store, bought a watermelon, and were found laughing in the backyard, watermelon juice smeared all over their faces.

"The point is," Sarah concluded, finally turning to look him in the eye, "we need to make time for each other. You're a good man, Ben Rosen, an excellent husband, and a hard worker, but we need time—time to be together, just you and I."

Ben sighed. "We will, we will. I promise." He squeezed her shoulders meaningfully as if that act alone concluded their conversation and began moving towards the door. It was 7:47. He was really late. He needed to leave immediately. He felt panic overwhelm him. However, for some reason he knew that he was forgetting something vital. He patted his pockets, making sure he had his keys and wallet. He did, but he did not feel right. He felt off-balance somehow. He went through a mental checklist of everything he needed—not just keys and wallet, but credit cards, pens, his watch, even shoes and socks and underwear—all the while letting his mouth talk, automatically, in sales mode.

"Thank you for your thoughts, Sarah," he said. "I think you are absolutely right. In fact I *know* you are right. We need to do something together, we really do. I'll make a note of that and get back to you. I just can't have this discussion now. I have to go. People are waiting. Important people."

And with that, he gave up his mental search and turned again towards the door to leave. Something whizzed by his head, crashing into the lamp beside him, denting the shade and knocking the base to the floor. A black plastic shingle, his cell phone, lay at his feet, miraculously still intact.

"Important people? Important people? Is that what you think of us, of me? That we are unimportant?" Ben looked up to see Sarah glaring at him, her still-moist eyes blazing.

"No I … I didn't mean that. I, uh… I just meant that I have to go. I just can't talk now." Ben was stunned. Sarah had never thrown anything at him before, much less his cell phone. He brushed off some imaginary dust and put the phone back safely into his pants pocket. He then looked up at Sarah, trying desperately to comprehend what this all meant.

"So what are you looking at? Go away. Get to your precious job. I have my job too, you know. I have lots of things to do as well. The school could not function without me—all those kids, all on the verge of obesity, all needing instructions on how to play volleyball and dodgeball and kickball and stuff." Sarah's voice trailed off. She seemed to be arguing with herself.

"Sarah, I'm sorry. I didn't mean …"

"You sure are. Now get out of here. Go prepare for your meeting with all these important people, and be sure to say hi to Bambi for me. I know you love talking to her."

Instantly Ben's sympathy turned to anger. Sarah had gone too far. "Her name is Bobbi, Sarah, and she is just my administrative assistant. Nothing more."

"Sure?"

"Sure."

"Fine then. Give her my best."

"I will."

"Fine."

"Fine."

Sorry, I Have to Take This

Driving to Work

> *Unfocused professionals often are distracted by e-mail, instant messaging, text messages, Twitter, pings, and other electronic media. After a while, they may feel that electronic devices are controlling them and not vice versa and that they're reacting rather than being proactive. Because of their reactive approach, they feel stressed out and have cluttered minds.*

After his "discussion" with Sarah, Ben welcomed the drive to work. He needed time to cool down. Even though he was late, he decided to take the long way through Indian Hill. An extended spin in his black Lexus SC 10 convertible was just what he needed to clear his head. He also needed time to figure out what he was going to say at this morning's meeting. He got in his Lexus, felt the soft leather seats enfold him, and immediately felt better. This was what he was up to; this was his future, their future—they were all speeding to success, and today he was about to shift into a higher gear.

Ben gripped the laminated steering wheel and started up the engine. Like a rocket, the 4.3 liter V8 engine came to life instantly, sending the illuminated needle bouncing in the tachometer as he revved it a few times. Ben checked the outside temperature, turned off the Mark Levinson sound system, and, shifting into reverse, punched the accelerator. The tires screeched as he left the garage. He hoped Sarah heard him. He was doing this for her, after all.

As soon as Ben got to the end of the driveway, he waited until Scott Fergusson was almost out of his driveway and then pressed the button to retract his hardtop. In 25 seconds the top was folded and stowed in the rear trunk. It was a thing of engineering beauty. Even Fergusson had to stop and admire it. So there, Mr. Classic Mustang.

Ben turned left out of his development and was able to open the Lexus up some on Wards Corner Road. The wind felt great in his hair. It made him feel like his troubles were being whisked out of his mind like so much litter. However, he still could not concentrate on his upcoming meeting. He kept thinking about Sarah and asking himself why was it that they always seemed to fight just before some important event at work? Didn't she see what these things meant? Didn't she see the sacrifices he was making, not just for him, but for the entire family?

Last year it was his trip to Seattle, probably the biggest moment in his entire career with DigitALL. Mr. Shaw himself had called him to headquarters to go over his new duties. It was a tremendous compliment, but it was also an opportunity for disaster. He had to be on top of every detail of his new assignment, or he would have been back on the street in a week. He wanted to be at Aaron's soccer games and support Amy in her gymnastics. It pained him, but he just couldn't. Too much was at stake.

And just last week when the Sears account was about to fall through, he had to spend extra time in Chicago mending fences and fixing all of the damage Jim McKenzie had done in over-promising what DigitALL's deluxe platinum plan involved. Jim was fired, of course, but relations with Sears still had to be restored, which meant loads of meetings involving network services, software support, computer setup, as well as marketing and legal—all of which had to be held in Chicago to show DigitALL's ongoing commitment.

And he did all this to save his family, along with his company, from financial oblivion. He was doing this for Sarah and the kids. He just did not understand Sarah's complaints about his being out of touch and sounding distant—and about his relationship with Bobbi.

Ben missed the green light at Branch Hill Guinea and sat at the intersection, listening to his engine and watching the steady stream of Fords, Chevys, and Dodges—mostly used cars—flow by. This area was domestic car country. It had been as long as he remembered it. His cell phone rang on the seat beside him, sounding the familiar "You're No Good" ring tone. He let his answering service pick it up. He did not need to. He already knew it was Sarah, supposedly calling to say she was sorry, but really demanding that he apologize—and talk.

Talk? Ben did not know what to say any more. Things were so different now. Sarah was so different. She used to just understand him. All through college, or at least since their junior year, they used to stay up late talking, just talking. Ben couldn't remember what they talked about. School maybe. Classes, professors, their ambitions, fears, dreams? Ben was not sure.

There was just something about being around her then that made him feel as if he could do anything, conquer the world if he wanted, even pass chemistry or crush Jimmy, Sarah's old boyfriend, in tennis. But now, now when he was actually conquering a small piece of the world, being around her made him feel small, as if he could do nothing right.

The light changed and Ben sped off, continuing down Wards Corner Road. The cell phone soon rang again. This time another ring tone sounded, a more upbeat "Smooth Operator." This call Ben took.

"Hey Bobbi."

"Hey Boss." No one else called Ben "Boss"—only Bobbi. In anyone else's mouth, the word sounded distancing, cold, superior even. But when Bobbi said it, it sounded like a nickname, better than "Benny" or Benj"—there was no mockery in it, just respect.

"I'm glad you called. I am going to be a little late this morning. Can you hold down the fort alone for a little while?"

"I don't know. The Indians are already circling, and Wilkinson already caught one arrow in his ... uh ... shoulder."

Ben forced a laugh and then did not say anything for several seconds.

"Are you okay, Boss?"

"Yeah, sure, Bobbi. I just got a late start today. That's all."

"It's just that you sound a little sad."

"Do I?"

"Yes."

Ben did not respond. He did not know what to say, what he could say. After a few seconds of awkward silence, Bobbi spoke up again.

"Well, it's obvious you don't want to talk about it. That's okay. Probably none of my business anyway. I just wanted to tell you the slides are all set for your presentation and ... well, that you are the best boss in the world."

"Thanks, Bobbi, but I am sure you have had others who were much better."

"No, no, not really." Bobbi then explained how most of her other employers had never asked her opinion about anything. She was just a "gopher," someone to fill in the gaps and do whatever the employer did not want or have the time to do. Ben just listened. The light had changed just ahead, at the intersection of I-275, and he slowed down, gliding to a stop. He thought about taking the beltway despite his original plan and zipping into work almost on time. Something about talking to Bobbi had made him feel better about things, about himself, and after all there was still so much he and Bobbi had to do before the meeting. However, just then the light changed, and more or less as a reflex Ben accelerated forward, away from I-275, and any chance of getting to work on time.

"So, anyway, you're different, Boss. You seem to value me as a person, as a contributing member of the team. So, thank you."

"No, thank *you*, Bobbi. I could not function without you."

"Really?"

"Really."

12

"So can I have the rest of the day off?"

This time Ben laughed easily. "No way. We have too much to do."

Bobbi laughed too. "Yes, I know. You haven't actually seen these charts, have you?"

"No, I wanted to review them over the weekend but our home computer caught a virus, and I could not access my e-mail. Why? Is something wrong?"

"Not exactly. It's just that … well, you'll see for yourself when you get in."

Ben was concerned. Bobbi was not usually this evasive. Something must really be wrong. He thought about asking her about it, but decided instead to let it go. There would be plenty of time to look over the slides once he got to the office. He knew things were not looking all that good last week, but a number of reps had promised him that several accounts would be coming in at the last minute. So the numbers were probably all right. Maybe the reports were incomplete or Lisa or another new rep had filled out the form wrong. In any case, it was probably something he had to see to understand. It could wait. He had plenty of time. Ben slowed as he approached the hill going down to Miamiville. "Okay, I'll be there shortly."

"Okay," Bobbi repeated playfully, mimicking his impatient tone. "See you soon."

"Okay." Ben said again, enjoying the joke.

"Okay. Oh, and Boss?"

"Yes, Bobbi?"

"You really are the best boss in the world despite what everyone else thinks."

Ben chuckled. "Thanks."

"Bye."

"Bye."

Ben hung up and wound his way down the hill, never touching the brakes once. Ben was always amazed at how the Lexus cornered. It seemed to sink into turns, gripping the road even tighter, hunkering down as it gained speed.

Ben zipped into the final curve at the bottom of the hill, and then slowed down as he entered Miamiville proper.

The Lexus slowed to near legal speeds. On the right, a farmer was hooking up what looked like a new baler to his tractor. Normally, Ben would have stopped just to see what make the baler was, but not today. Today Ben was still thinking about Bobbi and asking himself why he enjoyed talking to her so much. Was she really more connected to him and his life than Sarah? A shadow passed over the road. Was Sarah right? Was he losing interest in her? But then wasn't Sarah losing interest in him as well?

All Sarah seemed to want to talk about, when they did talk, was Derrick, her co-PE teacher at school—what new games he had invented, how he motivated the kids to get off their butts and move, and how he was setting up his own personal training business using Sarah as his first "client," photographer, and partner. Ben pushed down the clutch and revved his engine just to hear it roar. He did not like this plan with Derrick.

Miamiville

> *Something almost always happens to reactive professionals to show, in striking relief, how untenable their approach is. It may be a crisis at work or at home, in their personal or professional life, but whatever it is it reveals in no uncertain terms the precariousness of their world.*

By 8:26 Ben was well into the village of Miamiville, but his progress had slowed considerably. The Lexus was practically crawling now as he coasted past the vintage frame homes with their picket fences and huge spreading trees. Something about the place attracted Ben, although he was forever glad that he did not live there. It was so backward, so nineteenth century. He half expected a buggy to pull up next to him and honk its bulb horn. He stopped at the intersection of Wards Corner Road and Mill Street and waited for the traffic to clear. Again his phone rang. He leaned over to the passenger's side and picked up his phone. It was Jerry Walsh from Procter and Gamble.

"Let's see what Lisa has done this time," Ben muttered to himself. Ben clicked his phone on.

"Hey, Jerry. What's up?"

"Hey Ben, did you get the e-mail I sent you last night?"

"No, sorry, we had a problem with my home computer last night, and I couldn't access anything."

"Interesting. So even people who keep everyone else from getting hacked get hacked themselves?"

Ben laughed. "Yeah, well I don't have DigitALL service at home. If I did, this never would have happened."

"I know, Ben. I was just teasing. Actually, it's good to know that you have some skin in the game as it were—you know what network problems are like. Anyway, I had a question about that new e-mail system you guys install. I mean, it sounds good and all, but we can't afford even a 1% loss of data. Are you sure this transition will be completely seamless?"

"Jerry, it's always good to talk to you, and I very much value our relationship with your company, but Lisa's your rep now. You can't keep calling me directly. I have other responsibilities now." Ben inched the Lexus forward, straining to see the road to his left.

"I know, I know, Ben. But you always give me the straight scoop, and I'm not sure Lisa is … well, up to speed yet."

"What do you mean? I trained her myself." Ben opened his briefcase next to him, twisting his body, letting up ever so slightly on the brake. Not seeing the sheet he wanted, he started flipping through his papers, pushing the meeting plans aside, accidentally crumpling them.

"Well, last week, we were on the phone and I asked her …"

The truck seemed to come out of nowhere. It was like a dream, a bad dream. Ben remembered looking up and seeing something red—a dull blur that seemed to grow gradually larger and more distinct, until it finally filled his entire windshield. Time stopped.

Then, like a movie shown frame by frame, it started up again, clicking forward, ever so slowly.

The truck inching forward. Click.

An arm, clad in plaid, moving across his field of vision. Click.

Eyes, sky blue, staring at him. Click.

Growing wider and wider. Click.

Along with a mouth, a silent expression of surprise. Click.

It all went so slowly that for a moment Ben thought that he had missed it, that the red truck had passed by unharmed, sparing his Lexus by inches. But then, click, came the shudder, a sickeningly earthquake-like feeling, followed by the, click, gradual twisting of his car to the left and then, click, the slow puff as the airbag deployed, expanding into his face, knocking his arms aside and enveloping his face in white. His cell phone flying off into the unknown.

And then it was over.

"My Lexus," Ben screamed, "my beautiful Lexus." He shoved the airbag out of the way, pulled on the handle, and shouldered the car door open. Shaking his head, he stood up and leaned on the windshield as he surveyed the damage. He felt like someone had punched him in the gut. The hood looked okay but the left front fender had buckled, jamming it back into the tire. From where he was, he could not tell but he guessed that the HID Xenon headlight on that side was completely destroyed along with the front bumper cover and perhaps even the bumper itself. He groaned. This was going to cost a mint to fix, if it could be fixed at all. Steam hissed from the now open space between the hood and the grill. It looked to him like the end of the world.

"'Our inventions are wont to be pretty toys, which distract our attention from serious things.'"

Startled, Ben twisted around to see an old man, looking like he was in his sixties, grinning down on him, snickering from inside a truck, a truck too rusty to tell if its original color was red or that is just the way it was now. On the side was a scratched out "Mr. Termite" sign that had been painted over something else.

Above it, the man's long white hair partially obscured his unshaven face, which was resting on a flannelled arm, which in turn rested on the driver's side door. Everything about the guy seemed relaxed, calm, amused. Detached somehow, almost serene—everything Ben was not.

"Did you say something?" Ben asked tentatively. He still was not sure this was not a dream, a bad dream.

The old man brightened. "I sure did. It's a quotation from Thoreau. Do you like it? It means that you were talking on your cell phone when you should have been driving."

Caught off guard, Ben instinctively stepped back, crunching something under his foot. Ben looked down. It was his cell phone, now in pieces in the dust and gravel. He blushed and quickly kicked it under the car. "No, I wasn't."

"Sure you were," the old man replied, looking even more amused. "I saw it just as I made my turn. You were inching forward without realizing it. Your head was down. You were talking on your phone, while looking for something on the seat beside you, not paying the slightest bit of attention to what you were doing."

The old man cleared his throat noisily and spat, away from Ben. "Who was it anyway? Your wife? An important client? Your secretary? Ah, that's it. Your secretary. Your "work wife." Can't seem to talk to her enough, can you? You tell her everything, right? Your problems at work? Your problems at home? She is such a good listener. In fact, I bet you don't think you could function without her, right?"

"That's not how it happened," Ben protested, stung by the old man's near verbatim quotation of his own words.

The old man spat again. "Well, it's just as well. Relationships like that never work out, you know. They're desperate and, as Thoreau said, 'It is a characteristic of wisdom not to do desperate things.' He also said, 'Rather than love, than money, than fame, give me truth.' I really like that one too, especially today."

Ben's right hand balled up into a fist. He was not sure what irritated him more—the smugness of the guy, the way he kept quoting Thoreau, or the fact that he had just ruined his favorite car. Ben moved menacingly toward the truck.

"You wanna step out of that truck and say that, Mr. Termite?"

The old man did not budge. "I'm not Mr. Termite any more. There are too many stupid ideas in the world that need exterminating to waste my time killing bugs—or fighting with fools. But if you want to add assault to your other crimes, go ahead. I can handle anything a wannabe rich boy like you can dish out." The old man stuck out his head and offered his cheek to Ben.

Ben took a step back, confused. "What crimes? You ran into me."

The old man chuckled. "Nice try, son. Look down at your feet."

Ben looked down. Glass from the headlight was everywhere. A strip of chrome from his grill lay just to his right and the left wheel-cap was nowhere to be seen. Ben's heart sank. His poor Lexus.

"You see that large strip of white paint on the pavement? That is where the nose of your over-priced car should be. You ran into me, son—at least that is how the police are going to see it."

Ben looked again. The old man was right. Just below him, even with his seat back was a white line—worn, cracked, seemingly frayed a bit on the sides, but still clearly visible, glistening slightly like a small diving board. The Lexus was a good five feet into the intersection. Ben relaxed his fist and brought his hand to his face. He had no case. His insurance premiums were going to skyrocket. And he was going to have to pay for all of the repairs—for both vehicles. And there was the cost of the ticket. This was going to cost him a fortune. Suddenly, Ben brightened.

"Is there any way we can handle this without involving the police?" he asked.

The old man rubbed his bewhiskered face. "I don't see how. I mean, I heartily accept the motto, 'That government is best which governs least,' but someone's probably already called them. And besides, how do I know you will pay up?"

"Pay up? Your truck was hardly damaged. It's my car that took the hit."

Ben reached into his pocket and pulled out his wallet. He had six fifties in it, money he had ready in case he and some of the reps arrived early and he had to take them to breakfast. He held out four of them. "Here is two hundred dollars. Take it to repair your truck, and we'll call it even."

The old man did not move—his hand still on his chin. "You still think this is an accident, don't you? Some random event that did not have to happen? Some chance meeting of two vehicles that would not have occurred if somewhere in the universe some moth had wiggled its wings just one more time?"

The bills wilted in Ben's hand like lettuce. "Isn't it?"

"No. This is your chance, boy, your chance to wake up and take charge of your life. 'The mass of men lead lives of quiet desperation,' and no one is more desperate than you. Your desperation caused this wreck. It set up the circumstance and planned this conclusion. And it is desperation that is now causing you to speak nonsense. If you had been prepared—if you had known what you were going to do today and more importantly why you were doing it, you would not have been trying to fix things at the last minute or cover over your own stupid mistakes. You would have noticed not only my truck but everything around you."

The old man gestured vaguely towards something behind Ben. Ben turned to look, but there was nothing—just trees and shrubs and old houses. He then turned again towards the old men and was startled to see an old, boney index finger, pointed right at his nose, as if it were a pistol, as if it were loaded.

"But you are asleep—asleep, I tell you—lulled into unconsciousness by cell phones, beepers, pagers, laptops, GPS devices, and other technological whatsithoos that you think you are controlling but are controlling you. They are the danger. They keep you from seeing things as they really are. They brought you here and almost killed you. But you, like me, have escaped to tell the tale and if you don't learn from this experience and figure out how to control them, they will ultimately destroy you and everyone around you. Even your family. Especially your family. This is your chance, sleeper, your chance to change, to wake up, to see life as it really is, and to take charge. You have been warned. That is all I have to say."

And with that, the old man uncocked his finger, pulled his hand back into his truck, and drove off, glaring at him all the way. He did not go far, however, just off the road, into a gravel area on the other side of the road, still close to the corner but out of the way of traffic. Ben collapsed back into his Lexus. Not only had he had an argument with Sarah, wrecked his car, and smashed his cell phone, but now he had to pay for it all. AND he had to deal with Old Mac-loony as well. Ben glanced into his rearview mirror. The old man was now out of his truck, hacking away at the bushes beside his truck with a stick he had found somewhere.

"What a nut-case," Ben muttered to himself. "Probably an escapee from a convalescent home or something."

The thought gave Ben some hope momentarily. Maybe the old man has stolen the truck and was driving illegally. Maybe this would somehow be all his fault. However, after a few minutes of watching the guy and seeing how there seemed to be some method to his efforts, like he was clearing away weeds and not just randomly whacking away at them, Ben sank back into his seat and wallowed in his misery. After a few minutes, two pedestrians came by and asked him if he wanted their help to move his car off to the side. Ben did, and after he pulled his damaged fender away from the tire, together they pushed the Lexus out of the way, on the opposite side from the old man.

Sorry, I Have to Take This

Phil

> *At the time of a self-inflicted crisis, it helps to have a long-time friend, a trusted colleague, a business coach, or someone else who can help the professional see exactly what he or she is doing wrong and then explain the problem in terms that lead to a solution.*

A policeman, Officer Williams, showed up about 30 minutes later—not bad considering that this was a week day and it was still rush hour. He looked over the Lexus and spoke briefly with Ben, mostly to see if he was all right and to collect his license and registration information. Officer Williams then walked over to chat with the old man. In his rearview mirror, Ben could see them smiling and seemingly joking around. The officer even helped the old man move a branch that was sticking out of his now mostly cut down bushes. This was not good, thought Ben. Not only was he in the wrong, but now the crazy old man and the officer were buddies as well. He would be lucky not to end up in jail.

After a few minutes, the officer went back to his cruiser, pulled out two clipboards, and handed one to Ben.

"Just fill out the necessary insurance information and write down, as best you recall, what happened, okay?"

Ben nodded and took the clipboard. The officer then took the other clipboard to the old man. Ben did not watch the officer hand it to him or keep track of where the officer went afterwards. He concentrated on the form instead. He did not know what to say. He did not want to lie, but he did not want to pay for all this either. As a compromise, he wrote twice that he did not "think" that he had allowed his car to move forward and implied that the old man had been speeding. After all, Ben had not seen the truck at all and they had hit pretty hard—at least harder than Ben would have expected for someone turning into Wards Corner Road. He, of course, never mentioned the cell phone.

And it was a good piece of writing too, but Ben had little hope it would do any good. The evidence even after they had moved the vehicles was still pretty clear. And then there were witnesses too. Without feeling much hope, he handed the clipboard back to the officer and waited like a condemned man about to be sentenced.

But the expected verdict never came. The officer, all smiles and friendly, came back over to him after getting both statements, asked him for some additional information about his work—the address and phone number—and then said that Phil apologized for any inconvenience he had caused him by hitting his car. The officer then handed Ben the old man's insurance information with a business card. He explained that a full accident report would be available at the Miami Township Police station in three days and, in the meantime, he advised Ben to call the number on the card and arrange to get his car repaired as soon as possible. He also said that he had looked over the car and, although the radiator was leaking some, he thought he did not need a wrecker since he only had a few miles to get to his office. However, he advised him not to drive very long without checking it over thoroughly.

Ben was stunned. Out of reflex, he took the papers Officer Williams offered him and put them on the seat beside him, all the while staring uncomprehendingly at the officer's mirrored sunglasses. Ben's face looked huge and distorted, almost clownish in his confusion.

"The note on the card explains everything," the officer said, pointing to the seat beside Ben.

"Thanks," Ben responded, still dazed.

"Just read the card, and you'll know what to do."

"Oh, got it." Ben suddenly came to himself, reached over, picked up the card, and waved it to the officer.

"Read it."

"I will."

"Now."

"Okay." The front read simply "L. E. 'Phil' Fleischmann" with "Mr. Termite" struck through and "present in the present" printed at the bottom where the address normally appeared. Ben looked up at Officer Williams' glasses again. This was all so surreal. He had no idea what to make of the card or the words on it.

Officer Williams motioned for Ben to flip the card over. He did. On the back, scribbled in pencil was a note: "WE MUST LEARN TO REAWAKEN AND KEEP OURSELVES AWAKE. GOOD LUCK, SLEEPER. I ACCEPT ALL RESPONSIBLILTY. THIS IS THE CHANCE I WISH I HAD. MAKE THE MOST OF IT!" Then there was something that looked like a signature with a phone number under it.

"Any questions?"

Ben felt like kissing the guy. "So I just call this number and someone will fix my car? Completely? Without charge? Just like that?"

"Just like that," Officer Williams nodded.

"No insurance company? No report? Nothing?"

"No insurance company. No report. Nothing."

Ben's salesman brain kicked into gear. "What is the catch?"

"No catch. It is all taken care of and it is perfectly legal. Just call the number and your car will be fixed in a week. I don't expect any problems but if you have any, just contact me and I will personally take care of it. Or, if you prefer, you can go the standard insurance route. However, I think you will like the first way better. This guy does great work. In any case, the accident report will be available in a few days and the fact that Phil is fully responsible for all repairs is all legally documented. Anything else?"

"Yeah," Ben leaned in close, "what is 'L. E. Phil's' situation?"

Officer Williams smiled wryly and leaned in close, but before he could say anything his shoulder radio squawked. Something about a 10-50pi on corner of Cook and Cottontail. He reached over to his speaker, clicked something and said, "Got it. David111 responding." Then he turned back to Ben. "Sorry, it's a long story, and I have to go. Ask someone back at the department when you come in to see the report. Have a good day, sir." And with that the officer started to trot back to his cruiser. However, after a few steps, he stopped and went back to Ben.

"One more thing."

"What is that?"

"You are a very lucky man." And with that the officer, now running, returned to his cruiser and drove off, his lights flashing.

Ben sat in his Lexus, watching Officer Williams drive off, not quite knowing what to do. The whole thing was so unbelievable. He read the card in his hand again as well as the insurance information, clearly labeled, BACKUP, for clues. It was all there. It was true. Not only was he not getting a ticket, but all of his considerable repairs were being taken care of—and if they were not to his liking, he had a cop to make sure they were fixed. Ben raised his right hand to high-five someone, but, since no one else was there in the car with him, he slapped his rearview mirror lightly.

In the mirror, Ben could see that the old man, Phil, had already left. There was only gravel beside the bushes were his truck had been. He put his knee in his seat, stood up, and looked around. No rusty red truck anywhere. He plopped back down in his seat and looked again at the card the officer had left him. If it were not for that card, it would have been easy to dismiss the whole incident as a dream. It was so weird, so unreal. This could not have happened to him. But one look at the front of his car reminded him in very real terms that this had indeed happened.

Still, if this mechanic was good, perhaps it would not be a total loss. Perhaps the Lexus would be back in its usual shape. Maybe even with a new paint job. Ben had gotten tired of silver. He had seen a BMW on the Internet that was painted a stunning metallic green. Perhaps he could get this guy to repaint the Lexus metallic green. That would really impress his department. And green was a positive color too.

His department! The meeting!

He started up the Lexus and glanced at the illuminated clock on the dashboard. It was 9:27 am. He had not realized all this with the officer had taken nearly an hour. Without even thinking of testing things out, Ben slammed his car into gear and pealed out, sending dust, gravel, and the remnants of his cell phone shooting out behind him. Fortunately, no other cars were on the road just then and he did not cause another accident. In a few seconds, he was speeding along Mill Street, up Center Street, through Remington and into Indian Hill. He wished more than anything that he had not chosen to go this way today. Not only had he had the wreck, but everyone moved so much slower on these back roads. And they were all single lanes, so curvy and their sight lines so obscured by trees that passing was out of the question, even for Ben.

Still, Ben did the best he could, braking only slightly while going into curves and accelerating out of them. More than once he almost clipped a car that had wandered too close to the center line as he came out of a turn, and both times the driver had a cell phone clapped to his ear. Once a woman, stopped at the intersection of Remington Road and Montgomery Road refused to move, despite the green light. Ben sounded his horn long and loud and still only after a few more seconds did she begin to move forward. She too, Ben noticed, as he passed her on Montgomery, was talking on a cell phone. Perhaps Phil, as crazy as he was, was not wrong about the danger of cell phones on the road. Ben wondered why he had not noticed this before—perhaps it was because he had been using one himself.

In any case, Ben arrived at the office at 9:49—just enough time to talk with Bobbi and find out what is going on before the meeting started. The only problem was that several people, including Bobbi, had seen him drive up and were funneling out of the building to see the new condition of his car.

"Are you all right?" someone asked. "Did you hurt yourself?" "Are you okay?" "What happened to your car?"

Ben turned to look at his Lexus. Although it had not overheated, despite Ben's driving, some steam was coming out of the front.

"I'm okay," Ben said, loudly enough for everyone to hear, and turning around slowly so everyone could see. "I just bumped into a client on the way to work. That's all." Everyone laughed.

"Looks like it was a hard meeting," Sid said, patting him on the shoulders. "You look tired."

Not to be outdone—after all, he had minored in English—Ben laughed and pointed to the Lexus' front end, "Yeah, he really grilled me." Others shook his hand or otherwise expressed their relief that he was not hurt. Ben explained briefly what had happened and then added "But enough about me, we have a sales meeting to attend to. So let's get to it."

Still buzzing, everyone began filing back into the building, almost like the all clear had been sounded after a fire drill. Ben found Bobbi in the back, holding a sheaf of papers for him.

"I'm so glad you're okay, Boss. You really had us worried." She handed Ben the sheaf of papers and let her hand linger, ever so slightly, on his as he took them.

"I tried calling you, but your cell phone doesn't seem to be working."

Ben took the sheaf and started to look them over. "Sorry, I didn't mean to worry you. My phone was damaged in the collision. I couldn't call anyone. Are these the printouts of the slides?"

"Yes. I formatted them as usual and arranged them by area, the way you like them, but they are not at all what we expected."

Some of the reps bumped into Ben on their way into the building. "Wouldn't let a wreck get in the way of a sales meeting? Man, Ben, you are amazing." Ben smiled and said, "What did you expect? We can be thrown off track by every nutshell or mosquito's wing that falls on our path."

The reps forced a laugh and moved on. Ben turned again to Bobbi. She was smiling at him quizzically. "Where did that come from?"

"I don't really know. It just kind of popped out. Listen, I don't have time to go over the slides. I will just have to wing it until lunch. I'll have some time then to figure out what comes next."

Bobbi sighed. "Okay. But this is no insect body part we are talking about here. It is more like a piece of a space station that just landed in front of us."

Ben patted her on the arm. "I'll be all right. I've done this before. I'm in sales, remember? I can sell anything."

"Alright, if anyone can, you can. Do you want me to at least get you a sandwich or something?"

"Yes, that would be great." Ben started to leaf through the print-outs and then stopped. "Oh, and will you please call this number and find out if this place is legit?" Ben handed Phil's card to Bobbi. "They supposedly will fix my car quickly with no cost to me."

Bobbi took the card, flipped it over, and began reading the front. Ben noticed her skeptical look.

"It's a long story. I'll tell you about it later. Anyway," he shifted the sheaf of papers to his left hand, "wish me luck."

"Good luck, Boss," she responded, turning her attention back to him. She looked concerned. "You'll need it."

Ben started up the steps. "Oh, and I will need a new cell phone too."

"Got it," Bobbi replied and went back to her desk.

Sorry, I Have to Take This

The Big Meeting

One of the reasons businesspeople today often find it hard to focus on real relationships is that they increasingly rely on teleconferencing, webinars, and electronic communications as substitutes for face-to-face communication. While this approach may be cheaper in the short run, in the long run it destroys those relationships and causes these people to be out of touch with their colleagues and customers. They may think they are on top of the situation, but the reality is that they are far from it.

By the time Ben walked into the room, everyone was seated. The projector was on, ready to go, and the conference line was open. Tiny red lights glowed continuously over each mic. Ben wasted no time and started the meeting as he usually did—first by greeting everyone in the room by name—saying something about how he was glad to see them again and that they hadn't run into him on the road (polite laughter)—and then by acknowledging the others who were dialed in via the conference line.

Ben paused for a moment, taking in the room. He thought about the old man, Phil, and how vigorously the old coot had put down technology. But here in this room it was working marvelously. If only Phil could somehow see this sight. Half of the reps in his region were attending his meeting without actually being physically present—all because of the miracle of his "cursed" technology—and at a fraction of the cost. Because of this line and the ability they had to send out his slides over the web in real time, only about six reps had to deal with the hassle of airports, rental cars, hotels, and finding their way to this building—although here again GPS devices could help with that.

Wake up, Sleeper? It was Phil who was asleep, totally unconscious of the benefits of cell phones and computers and all the other electronic things he derided. In the past, they had always had some remote attendees—mostly one or two reps who could not come to Cincinnati because of health or some other issue. Ben had Bobbi e-mail them his presentation, and they clicked along as best they could, all while listening in on the phone. However, now the reps could actually see his presentation and even participate. He could also make last-minute changes and even adlib if he wanted to. There was no practical reason they had to physically attend the meeting, and therefore many of the reps just dialed in.

Ben put Phil out of his mind and confidently concentrated on the matters at hand. He looked down at the star-like conference phone and joked about how much better the remote reps looked these days—their tans were coming along (the conference phone was light brown) and they all looked like they had lost some weight (the four "arms" of the phone, where the mics were located, were fairly narrow and sleek-looking—almost like something from *Star Trek*). More polite laughter filled the room and sounded sporadically over the line. Ben felt progress fill the room like oxygen. They were all boldly going forward.

"Well, that went over well," Ben said, laughing at himself, and, then turned his attention back to the six reps who were actually in the room. He rubbed his hands together and suggested they all get down to the business at hand, starting with status. His plan was to press on with this first part of the meeting and wait for something to present itself as a theme or direction for the next part. There was no need to worry with this group. They were so engaged and creative that something always came up. Sometimes he had to tone down their humor a bit and refocus them occasionally, but most of the time he just let them go at it. His job, as he saw it, was to keep everything positive at least on the surface. That was what he had discovered fairly early on—make things look good and usually they turn out that way in the end.

However, as soon as Ben showed the first slide, he knew he was in trouble. As usual Bobbi had done a wonderful job of making the slides look professional. The template was carefully chosen, with colors that were appropriately coordinated and upbeat. She had chosen a font that was both distinctive and readable, and the animation contributed to the presentation without distracting from its content. However, that was the problem—the content. It quickly took the gloss off of the charts, at least for Ben.

It was much worse than he had expected. Slide after slide, chart after chart, the trends were unmistakable. Nothing had come through at the last minute and, from the looks of it, some of the gains he had seen in the weeks previous had been reversed—probably an accounting irregularity. No matter how slick the 3-D graphs were arranged—oftentimes using large units to minimize the delta from month to month—they could not disguise the trouble they were in. Not even the occasional clip-art that Bobbi uncharacteristically threw in to lighten the mood helped. What Ben saw was not second quarter status but the end of the world. Everything was down from last quarter and down dramatically.

With every slide, Ben felt the burden on his shoulders increase almost as though someone were stacking bricks on him, one by one, pressing him down. After about an hour of this, Ben mustered enough courage to look away from the slide he was showing to the faces of the reps that were in the room with him. He braced himself for the ashen looks of terror and disgust he expected to see.

However, that was not what he saw. Instead he saw men and women who did not seem aware at all with what he was showing them. As he continued to talk, they fiddled with their cell phones. Most were texting or perhaps checking their messages, but some had actually turned away from him and were taking calls, their free hands held against their ears so that they could hear better.

Ben, confused by what he was seeing, paused momentarily, gathering his thoughts. Apparently several people on the conference line had failed to mute their microphones as they went about their business. He heard someone making lunch plans apparently with an office-mate or someone else who had dropped by. Another rep was typing something so furiously that the sound of the keys reminded Ben of rain, drenching his parade.

He tried to ignore the noise and pushed through several more slides. However, when the fanfare sounded announcing that someone had completed a game of Spider Solitaire, he gave up. He just stopped talking. Part of him wanted to see if anyone would notice and part of him just could not think of anything else to say. For what seemed like several minutes, no one said anything. The only sounds were the continuing cloudburst of typing and the whooshing of whispered conversations.

Ben tried his best to somehow project anger though his silence, almost as though through his pores, but no one seemed to notice or care. He could actually feel himself shrinking, growing smaller, less significant with each second. He had to do something. He had to say something. His and everyone's future depended upon it.

"Okay, you've been a good audience, and this is a good place to stop. Let's go to lunch a little early, but be sure to be back here at one. Okay?"

This everyone heard, even the remote reps. Almost instantly, all the typing and whispering stopped, and the room was deserted, except for Ben.

Ben turned away from the still projected slide, the graphic portrayal of his failure, and looked over the empty room. Until now, this had been his favorite room in the entire building—even more than his office. Here were all the plaques commemorating his success. Along the far wall, the "Wall of Fame," were the "Million Dollars in Sales" plaques from 1991 until 2010 arranged in three neat rows, with the names of the award winners engraved on them. "Benjamin B. Rosen" appeared on eight.

Next to the plaques was a kind of corner display shelf with some of the smaller awards in it, most of which Ben had also won—some more than once. There was the gold-plated top for "Top Rookie Salesperson of the Year." Check. The crystal car, a Corvette, for most miles logged while visiting customers. Two checks. The silver clock, its hands stuck at 12:01, for quickest sale of the year. Five checks. The surprise box, a recognition for surprising everyone by taking on a non-productive territory and, against all expectations, making it productive. No check. Ben had yet to win that one.

Ben walked over to the awards shelf and picked up the surprise box. Although made of carved wood, it was lighter than he had expected. He fiddled with the lid, and it unexpectedly came off—the ribbons being taped on to only look like they were connected. Ben stared at the emptiness inside. It was full of nothing but stale air.

Is that what I am? he asked himself. He had so wanted to win this award, the last on the shelf, but why? Was Phil right? Was he really asleep—just following the track laid out for him, a track that sometimes worked out but, like today, led him also to crashes over which he had no control? Was he really a desperate man doing desperate things for desperate reasons? Ben frowned, thinking of that old man shaking his boney finger at him and warning him, like some crazed ghost out of a Dickens' story—Jacob Marley in a baseball hat. Ben put the box back together and replaced it on the shelf.

No. He was not asleep and this was no desperate dream. This was real—too real, in fact. Ben closed his eyes, trying to rid himself temporarily of the pain he was feeling. He thought again about the day Mr. Shaw had given him this assignment. It was mid-October, last year, two weeks before Halloween. Mr. Shaw had flown him all the way to Seattle, put him up in a Hilton, taken him out to dinner, and, then, afterwards, in his office, congratulated Ben again on the work he had done in the Cincinnati-Northern Kentucky area. Ben felt like a million bucks that day, resplendent in

35

his new suit and shoes. He felt valued, important, powerful, like he could do anything.

Mr. Shaw then told Ben that he wanted him to similarly lift the entire Midwest/Great Lakes sales region. He winked at him. Yes, he smiled, he was promoting him, but then he grew very serious. He wanted Ben to know that he was not just giving him a new title—he was giving him a specific task, a quest, a CHALLENGE—for Mr. Shaw that word was always in uppercase letters, lit up in neon, blinking even, almost as bright as the light in his eyes were when he used it.

Mr. Shaw threw down that word like a gauntlet. He wanted Ben in a year's time to turn this troubled region around, to make it not just average but exceptional, one of the most productive regions in the company—to surprise him, in other words. Mr. Shaw even looked at the surprise box he kept in his office.

Ben started to say something. He was not unprepared, after all. He knew the job was opening up and he had heard there was only one reason Mr. Shaw flew people out to see him. If you were in trouble, he always came to see you—that's when Mr. Shaw the Mysterious became Mr. Shaw the Malicious, someone to be feared.

"I, uh, well ..." Ben began, trying his best to sound surprised. But Mr. Shaw held up his hand, stopping him before he could get started. He had a twinkle in his eye.

"And to sweeten the deal, I made a bet."

"A bet, sir?"

"Yes, a bet. You know Brian Jennings, our CFO?"

Ben nodded. Ben had heard Brian present a few times and had chatted with him afterwards. For some reason, he got the impression Brian did not like him.

"Well, Brian is a funny guy, an excellent man with numbers but he gets a bit stuck in his ways sometimes, and when we discussed this change as a group, Brian voted against it. He said that you were too young, too inexperienced, and too reactive to lead a group like this. He favored a more seasoned person. I, obviously, disagreed, and we argued about this for a good half hour."

Mr. Shaw looked at Ben, seemingly searching for a reaction. Ben did his best to remain stone-faced. He was not sure what this was leading up to. Mr. Shaw was famous for saying things just to rattle people, to keep them guessing. He had a reputation for being a man of misdirection, of mystery. This could be one of those times.

"Anyway, I finally proposed a bet. 'Okay,' I said, 'if you are so certain Ben can't do it, are you willing to bet your job on it?' I knew I had him then. Brian has a fine mind for business, but he is stubborn. He'll never retreat from a position once he had laid it out unless he is somehow conquered by overwhelming evidence, which I did not have. I am going just on an informed hunch here. 'Sure,' he said. And so I proposed that we promote you to this position and give you a year from now to transform the Midwest Region into the top sales region. If you did it, well then, he would retire."

"And did he accept?"

"Of course he did. Like I said, Brian is nothing if not stubborn, and I had him cornered. Actually, Brian needs to retire anyway. His health is failing him, and he needs to relax more. I had talked to him about retiring before, but, as I said …"

"I know, Brian is stubborn."

"Yes, you have the idea. So," Mr. Shaw looked him in the eye, "so, will you take the CHALLENGE? Will you help me win my bet?"

Ben snapped to attention. Something about being in Mr. Shaw's presence made him feel like he was in the military, and right now he felt he was being sent off to parachute behind enemy lines, take out their guns, and end the war for good. One of his colleagues even gave this feeling a name. He called it being "Shawed."

"I will, sir," Ben found himself saying. "Yes, sir. I'll make the Midwest region the best in the company."

"Excellent, excellent," Mr. Shaw said, taking his hand firmly. "Take 'the Pit' and make it into 'the Pinnacle.'"

Mr. Shaw held on to Ben's hand longer than usual, looking deeply into his eyes, seemingly pressing all of his strength into him. Then he let go, abruptly, suddenly, and walked back around to his desk, seemingly looking for something he'd lost.

"Okay. I'll send out a memo announcing the change this afternoon." Finding what he was looking for, a piece of paper, Mr. Shaw sat down and began to look it over—apparently unaware that Ben was still in the room.

Ben stood in front of his desk, not knowing what to do. Should he leave or did that paper have something to do with him? Ben shuffled his feet and finally coughed.

"Oh Ben," Mr. Shaw exclaimed, startled. "I thought you'd be halfway to Cincinnati by now, already turning things upside down. Anyway, it is good that you are here. I forgot to mention the other part of our bet."

"The other part?" Ben did not like Mr. Shaw's tone. It sounded ominous.

"If you don't turn the Midwest Region around, you lose your job."

Ben stared at Mr. Shaw, unable to discern if he was kidding or not. "My job?"

"Yes, your job." Ben again was not sure how to react. The whole idea of this bet seemed, well, childish to Ben—like something little boys would engage in. Certainly not something leaders of successful corporations would do. But Mr. Shaw just nodded, his expression as serious as a stone cliff. For a split second, Ben was not sure he wanted this job. This was a lot of pressure. He even thought about declining it.

But then, the stone cliff cracked and Mr. Shaw's face relaxed into a smile. "Gotcha."

Ben laughed partly out of relief, partly out of reflex. "Thank you again, Mr. Shaw. I won't let you down." He picked up his things and turned to go.

"You better not." Ben looked again up at Mr. Shaw, searching for some clue as to what he really meant. Ben found none. Mr. Shaw's eyes were now averted as he searched for something in his desk. Ben went along with what he assumed to be a joke, and left the room laughing. However, he could not shake the feeling that Mr. Shaw was joking about joking—that he was actually serious about firing him if his department was not number one in a year's time.

Anyhow, Ben was determined not to take the chance. He worked very hard and made substantial progress, even exceeding his numbers during his first two quarters in his new job. This was not as difficult as it sounded. Because the department had done so poorly the previous years, he had been given easier but graduated numbers. They were not yet the top region in the company, but they were no longer the worst. They had already passed most of the lower performing regions and were starting to threaten some of the historically more productive regions—like the Southeast/Atlantic region and Northeast/New England. Ben felt that with a strong performance in this year's second quarter, they could even be a position to worry California/Silicon, the perennial top performer.

But that had not happened. Second quarter had been a disaster. Not only had they not met their numbers, but given what he had heard from the other VPs, he was sure they had lost significant ground relative to other regions. And suddenly Mr. Shaw's bet—more of a threat than an actual wager—loomed large in Ben's memory. He had to think of something. Something had to change and change quickly.

Reflexively, Ben clenched his fists, thinking about how he was letting down the company, his family, and Mr. Shaw. His right hand closed on something deep in his pants pocket, something paper-like but stiffer. It bit into his hand. He pulled the thing out and looked at it.

It was L.E. "Phil" Fleischmann's so-called business card. He read again the words, "present in the present." Suddenly he had an idea. Phil may be a demented old hippy who could not drive his truck more than two feet without hitting something, but maybe he was on to something. Ben looked at his watch. He had about 45 minutes before the meeting resumed—just enough time to prepare his surprise.

Ben's Surprise

The first step towards "curing" insufficient focus is to buy into the idea that single-tasking has merit and that multi-tasking doesn't work. The second step in this process is to begin to lessen or at least control the digital devices that encourage multi-tasking and to promote single-tasking in relationships and activities.

When the reps returned, they found Ben at his usual place at the head of the conference table, smiling broadly with the surprise box centered directly in front of him. They took their seats quickly and resumed the conference call.

"Welcome to the second half of our meeting, ladies and gentlemen. Are you ready to rumble?" Ben began, doing his best to sound like a wrestling announcer. For an instant all the reps looked up at him. "This afternoon I have a surprise for you." He then picked up the surprise box and immediately saw the reps reach for their phones. The surprise box was not really a surprise for them. Ben's predecessor had used it several times before. However, Ben's approach was significantly different.

"This surprise is really a present. But it is a present that you both give as well as receive." Ben could see a few cell phones go down. He could tell that the reps were uneasy with this new development. This was not the usual way the surprise box was presented.

"Actually, I call it 'The Present of Presence,'" and Ben opened a new slide in the middle of his presentation and typed the phrase in the title box, in large letters, to make sure everyone, even those online, could see what he meant and would not confuse "presents" with "presence." He then removed the top of the box and instructed those present to place their cell phones in the box. They hesitated.

"Is this like a raffle?" Sid Brueggemann asked, holding his phone close.

"Yeah," someone else said, "does the winner get all the phones?" Most of the reps were laughing but their laughter seemed forced, too loud and too sporadic to be real. Ben could tell they were hoping they did not have to comply.

"Come on now. Put them all in the box," he said, thinking about Mr. Shaw and the way he always seemed convinced of the correctness of whatever he did. "This goes for those of you on the line too. Put your phones in a desk drawer or somewhere else where you cannot see them or hear them." Ben looked at the reps in the room until they eventually did as he requested. After a few agonizing moments, all the reps put their phones in the box, and all eyes were on Ben.

"Are all the phones put away?" he asked in the mic. "Everyone?"

"Yes," came several unenthusiastic electronic replies. "Okay, I am going to put the lid on the box and return it to the shelf now. Our phones are now out of our sight and out of our minds."

Ben then did so and went back to his seat. He just looked at the reps for a few seconds. There was only silence on the conference line. They were all bright, eager folks, the kind of people he would like having over to his home for dinner. He realized that he liked them. He really liked them—well, most of them—but he did not like the work they were doing, all of them, including himself. Finally he looked down at his hands. "What are we doing here?"

The words came out more tired, sadder than Ben had intended them. Sid started to tell a joke, but Carmen hushed him. Everyone went quiet.

"What do you mean, Ben?" Jason eventually asked. "What are we doing on earth?" Sid snickered. And again Carmen cut him short and whispered, "Ben has had a hard day today. He really loved that car."

Ben's Surprise

"No, that is not it, Carmen," Ben interrupted, "but thank you for your concern. The problem is that we are in trouble. Sales are down and our prospects are down. We are just not coming close to meeting our targets. We are in trouble and I mean big trouble."

Everyone seemed stunned. "Come on, Ben. It's not all that bad. We've seen worse quarters."

"Let's look at a slide again." Ben randomly clicked one of the slides—the Pittsburgh chart, from Steve Mitchell's area. He then went to the last slide, the composite Bobbi had created to show the overall progress, or lack thereof, of the department. There in vivid blue and pink and orange and red and violet, all the arrows pointed down, descending like bolts from above, unmistakable portents of absolute destruction. They stared at the graph as if for the first time, its meaning finally getting through to them.

"Wow," Jason said, speaking for everyone. "We *are* in trouble."

"Yes," Ben emphatically agreed. "We are."

The group remained silent for what seemed like several minutes, seemingly transfixed. Finally Steve turned to Ben and asked, "Okay, what do we do?"

Ben looked Steve in the eye. "I don't know." Again the group was silent.

Finally Lateesha Burton said something over the phone, the emotion in her voice amplified by the speaker. "What do you mean, 'You don't know?' You're the boss, the sales hotshot, the man with the answers."

Ben was ready. He folded his fingers together, forming a steeple with his index fingers, and said slowly. "Well, I know that is how it is supposed to be, but I am telling you I don't know what to do. I don't have the answers because I don't know what the problem is. That is why I asked what we are doing here."

"I thought we were having a meeting," Sean said, his young voice cracking, going up sharply at the end. It was just too much. Everyone laughed, even Ben.

"Yeah," Ben finally said, when everyone finally calmed down. "That was what I was afraid of—we were just having a meeting, looking at charts, sipping our coffee, checking our messages, just going through the motions. We can't do that today. We have to figure out what the problem is and find a way to address it."

"Excuse me," Robin, piped up, "but hasn't Corporate already told us what we are to do?"

Ben nodded affirmatively, and then remembering that she could not see him, he added, "Yep, make this area productive or hit the road." Those in the room laughed nervously.

"That was all? That was it?" Robin sounded incredulous, even somewhat betrayed. Her typing had stopped.

"You don't know much about Corporate, do you, Robin?" Sid said, the room again chuckling.

"I think I know more than you do," Robin responded, her voice sounding decidedly icy. Her typing then continued at a much accelerated pace. Ben could only imagine what she was saying to her buddies in headquarters.

Lateesha, still exasperated, voiced what Robin was probably typing. "So if this is such old news, how come you waited until now to tell us all this?"

Ben bit his lip. Be positive, he kept telling himself. Bringing up their lack of attention would not help anything. "I guess the full reality of what we were up against only recently dawned on me."

He then began typing in the text box below the words "The Present of Presence." The words "Any suggestions?" and "What's the problem?" appeared on the screen.

Answers came like an avalanche, all at once, with people talking over and around each other: the economic downturn, fear of the future, unwillingness to invest, a bad winter, the shift in regional demographics, unreasonable customer requests, unfair business practices on the part of their competitors, lack of information from development, too aggressive product expectations, too lenient product

Ben's Surprise

expectations, new assignments, change in corporate leadership, and so forth.

One rep, Jason Mueller, even suggested that gluten was somehow the cause of it all. Everyone in unison said "gluten?" and wanted him to explain. Ben, however, simply called the idea "interesting," and moved on.

"People, all—well, most—of these problems affect us, but they are not *our* problems. We cannot control them. We cannot solve them. They are excuses. What are our problems?"

The group went immediately silent, seemingly puzzled, wondering what Ben was getting at. Finally Sean raised his hand, almost as he was back in school again.

"Yes, Sean."

"I'm probably wrong, but isn't the problem the fact that we are not selling enough services?"

Everyone looked at Sean, ready to laugh but not quite sure if they should.

"Give that boy an A+," Ben bellowed. "That is exactly right. That is our problem. It's not a matter of the economy or our competitors or development or even gluten." Ben smiled at Jason and winked. "The problem is we are not selling enough services."

"Okay, what do we do about it?" Sid said, slapping the table. "Have a fire sale? Two service calls for the price of one?"

"That's an idea." Ben deleted all their previously mentioned "problems" and typed "Sell more services." It appeared large on the screen, like a mandate from heaven. Under it he started a bulleted list with "Have a sale" as the first item.

With that more ideas came in—technology fairs, a new sales award, more advertising, more sales personnel, telemarketing, TV spots, Internet promotions, better packaging. Ben was amazed at the number as well as the variety of the suggestions the group produced once he had their attention.

"All of these ideas are good solid ideas that undoubtedly can help," Ben said after his list had filled the screen. "The problem we have is that we have a little over two and a half months to change things around. Is there anything we can do quickly?"

Again the group fell silent. Finally, Radhika, who had not said anything so far, raised her hand.

"You don't have to raise your hand, Radhika. You're not Sean," Ben joked. Everyone laughed, even Sean. Things were going well. Everyone seemed engaged—even the folks on the phone.

"Sorry, I still feel pretty new here. I am not sure how things are done in this company."

"Just like your average kindergarten," Ben quipped, instantly regretting his use of the word "your." He had not meant to imply that she was five-year old. Actually, he was quite impressed with Radhika and her technical knowledge.

Radhika did not seem to notice. "Well, you all probably already do this, but since I just joined DigitALL, I did not receive my cell for more than a week and so I decided to visit our customers in Louisville. However, since I was so new and could not call you because I did not have a cell phone, I ended up visiting former customers, people who no longer used our services."

This produced a general laugh.

"Yes, it was embarrassing, but the odd thing was that many of them were glad to see me. They gave me the grand tour of their facility and a few even took me to lunch. They said our competitors never came by after they switched or seemed interested in their problems and ideas. They were impressed that I spent time with them and expressed an interest in switching back. Two already did."

"Man, are you lucky," Brueggemann exclaimed.

"Yeah, that would never work in the Twin Cities," John Mueller added. "Once they switch there, they switch."

Ben felt his moment arrive. "Are you sure?"

"Well, yes," John said, suddenly defensive. "Once Minnesota Mills went with one of our competitors, they never returned my calls or answered my e-mails. As far as they were concerned, I no longer existed."

"Yes, but did you ever actually visit them?"

"You mean, drive to their building, meet with the receptionist, walk up to an office, and ask to see them?"

"Yes."

"Well, No, I did not. I am not as lucky or as good-looking as Radhika here. No one wants to see me."

"Are you sure?" Lateesha said, batting her long eyelashes at John. "Some of us really like bald, uni-browed men with mismatched socks." Everyone laughed.

"My socks do too match," John said, trying to smile but still brushing back his few remaining hairs.

Ben pressed the point. "The fact is you really don't know. None of us does. And it took this exceptional rookie," Ben nodded towards a now thoroughly embarrassed Radhika, "to show us what we need to do."

He highlighted "The Present of Presence," increased its font size, and changed its color to red. "What I originally meant by this phrase was that we all needed to give each other the gift of our undivided attention as we attempted to solve this problem. However, together we have expanded the meaning of this phrase beyond what I had intended it to be. Together we have come up with a solid strategy to reach our goal."

"So, along with everything else you usually do," Ben smiled, "This month I want you to personally visit every former DigitALL customer in your area and get to know their current situation. Obviously try to make an appointment, but if you can't, just show up. Tell them you are doing research—checking up on well-run companies. Show interest. Take notes. Establish real personal relationships. And let's see where it leads. Okay?"

"Okay," they all agreed.

"Again, this is not just a request. This is an official department direction, an assignment, which I will be tracking and talking with you about in our weekly calls. I don't know. Let's call it, 'the Personal Attention Initiative.'"

"PAttI?" Sid quipped. "Come on, we can do better than that. That sounds like something from *Peanuts*."

"What?"

"You know, Peppermint Patti, the girl who calls Charlie Brown 'Chuck.'"

Everyone laughed—except for Ben. Things had been going well, but now he felt them slipping away from him.

"How about 'Face-to-Face?'" John suggested. "I mean, that is what we are doing, right? Meeting our customers face-to-face."

A few of the reps nodded in agreement.

"I like that," Ben said and typed "Face2Face" on his laptop. The words shone bold on the screen, glistening with hope.

"All in favor?" The room echoed with "ayes." "Anyone opposed?" Nothing.

"Okay, and with that the motion officially carries. 'Face2Face' it is. Now all we have to do is implement it. So, let's get to it," Ben said with finality. "Meeting adjourned."

But no one moved.

"Well, what are you waiting for?" he asked, confused. "Time's a wasting."

Still no one budged. They just stared at Ben, as though they were waiting for something. Finally, Radhika cleared her throat and asked very politely if they could please have their phones back.

Ben laughed. "Another brilliant insight from our rising star. Sorry." Ben then retrieved the surprise box, returned the cell phones to those in the room, and everyone left.

AFTER THE MEETING

> *After putting in place a single-tasking system, next make specific, written personal commitments to concentrate fully on each single task or interaction with a clean desk, a clear mind, and a clear purpose. Commit to focus directly on the person or activity in front of you.*

After the meeting, the reps who were staying in town for the night invited Ben to join them for dinner, their treat, and to discuss their plans to contact former clients. Ben was impressed by their enthusiasm and flattered that they had invited him. However, he told them he had plans. They pressed him to just join them for a drink, and again he begged off, citing his need to make sure his car would be taken care of. All of this was true, but the real reason Ben did not go was that he just wanted to bask in the afterglow of the meeting for a moment. They therefore went off by themselves, laughing and thanking Ben again for such a fine meeting.

Ben thanked them in turn and then closed the door after them. He turned off the projector, took a seat at the end of the table, closed his eyes, and, for the moment, just breathed. He was both elated and exhausted. He had never been to such a productive meeting before—certainly not one that he had conducted. In his mind's eye he visualized the discussion, the way people leaned forward and seemed eager to hear what the other was saying. He inhaled the lingering smell of their unified effort and their earnest commitment. It was almost intoxicating. It was as though the department, for once, was unified and moving forward together as a group.

And the mood was so easy to produce. Without cell phones or other distractions, everyone was actually paying attention, and they were engaged, really engaged. Ben opened his eyes and looked again at Phil's business card. "You were right, L.E. Phil, you sly fool," Ben said out loud. "Sometimes our inventions can be distractions."

He then pulled his laptop towards him, opened a Word document, and began typing using bold letters:

Rules for Avoiding Digital Distractions

Rule 1: Actually attend all meetings. This means more than just being physically present; it means being mentally present as well—focusing exclusively on the issues at hand and bringing to bear all of your faculties on those issues. You should therefore not be typing, sending e-mails, texting, checking messages or in any way using a cell phone during a meeting. In fact, cell phones are not allowed in meetings. Focusing in this way will ensure shorter, better, and more productive meetings.

Ben looked over what he had written. It was not exactly the Declaration of Independence, but it seemed to him like his English professors would have liked it anyway. It felt like an official pronouncement of some sort, the start of something big, something revolutionary, something that was going to change his world and save his neck to boot. He also typed out the strategy they had come up with, not in bold, and added a few observations of his own.

Ben saved the document and closed his laptop. This was great stuff. What a great day it had been. What a surprisingly great day, especially considering how it had started. He saw an umbrella that someone had left in the corner, walked over, grabbed it, hefted it in his hands, and then, on impulse, began dancing around the room singing "Step in Time" from *Mary Poppins,* one of his kids' favorite movies. He do-si-doed around the chairs, twirled the umbrella over the table, even clicked his heels in front of the awards shelf—all the while singing "Never need a reason, Never need a rhyme, Kick your knees up, Step in time!"

He was happy. He was a "sales sweep" cleaning up "the Pit" for Mr. Shaw and the company—helping his department dust off their old approaches, jumping over bureaucratic hurdles, twisting around self-imposed barriers, cart-wheeling their way into their customers' hearts and pocketbooks.

Just then Bobbi opened the door and peeked in. Ben froze mid-step, his right foot still dangling in the air after a particularly high kick. "Ben? Are you all right?" she asked tentatively. "I heard some noise."

Ben felt his face blush, but he resumed his dance anyway, without the singing. "All right? I am awesome!" He moved about the room rhythmically going "round the chimney" (actually, a chair) and "up on the railing" (more like two boxes of printer paper someone had left in the room), all the while looking directly at her. At one point Ben moved toward Bobbi and tried to entice her to "flap like a birdie," but she declined, holding tightly onto the door handle with both hands.

Finally Ben stopped and, leaning over, tried to catch his breath.

"So, I take it the meeting was a success?" Bobbi asked with a smile.

"Oh yes," Ben responded, panting. "Couldn't have been better."

"And the slides? Were they all right?"

Ben took hold of her forearms, and looked her in the eye. "They were awesome. Just awesome. The meeting was awesome. Everything was … awesome!" He pumped his fist for emphasis. "Thank you for putting it all together and for doing such a great job."

Bobbi looked pleased but still somewhat confused. She reluctantly returned his hold on her arms. "I don't understand, Boss. The trends were terrible. Everything pointed down. I thought you would be upset."

"I was and they were, but then everything changed. It was a miracle. It was like divine intervention." Ben then proceeded to tell her all about the first part of the meeting—his shock at the slides, their unrelenting bad news, and the obliviousness of the reps. He gesticulated wildly and paced about the room. He was no longer dancing but he could not seem to sit still. Bobbi followed him as he moved.

Finally Ben ended up in front of the awards shelf and reached for the surprise box. He handed it to her. "This was the key. This is what changed everything."

"The surprise box?" She twisted it around a few times and then, apparently unimpressed, set it down on the table. "This old thing. But there's nothing in it."

Ben took it up again. "Yes, there is ... er, was. I had them all put their cell phones in it and told the reps on the line to similarly stash their phones away, and once that was done, poof! Great things just started happening. It was like magic. Everyone paid attention, everyone participated. It was like we were all on the same page, the same sentence even—all joined together in one cause, pooling all of our thoughts and experiences to find a way to reach our goal. I could not have asked for a happier surprise."

Bobbi smiled broadly, her eyes almost closed with joy. "Oh, I am so relieved, Ben. I thought for sure the meeting would be a disaster and that you would come out of it sad and depressed. I am so happy that it worked out." She then came up to him and hugged him, around his arms, constricting them tightly against his body. Helpless, Ben felt her vanilla-scented perfume enfold him, like an intoxicating cloud, her strength and softness all around. He was both delighted and concerned.

Ben patted the lower part of her back awkwardly, unable to move, hoping she would let go quickly, but when she did not, he twisted out of her hold and stepped back away from her. "Er, thanks, Bobbi. Yes, it worked out—it worked out just fine. Thank you very much."

"I'm so glad," she said, still smiling, moving towards him again, her face coming within inches of his. "You are the best boss ever, and you work so hard. You deserve to have great things happen to you, and I am sure they will. This sounds like a great approach. Who else would have thought of it? It is so genius."

"So genius," Ben repeated as he turned away from her and modestly deflected her praise to the department as a whole, citing their contribution and admitting that he could not have come up with the idea all by himself.

"But you enabled them," she persisted, grabbing his shirt sleeve and twisting him back towards her. "You encouraged them. You encourage me." Bobbi looked for all the world like she was about to kiss him, but Ben quickly placed the surprise box awkwardly between them, blocking any further forward movement she may have had in mind. "And let's not forget this box. It helped a lot too."

Unfazed, Bobbi stuck out her hand. "I'm sure it did. But you are still the man, at least as I see it." Ben took her hand reluctantly. It was about the same size as Sarah's, only younger, smoother, and her nails were more elegant. Sarah, the P.E. teacher, always had torn up nails and small bruises on her arms. Bobbi shook his hand firmly. She was also stronger than Sarah. Bobbi then let go and raised her hand high, waiting apparently for a high-five. Ben obliged her, but he slapped her hand so lightly that it barely made a noise.

Bobbi grimaced. "That's no high-five. Try again. Gimme ten." She held both of her hands up, an action that presented her squarely in front of Ben and highlighted her shapely figure. Ben obliged her and even smacked her hands vigorously. However, he did so more as a push than a slap and knocked her back a few steps, away from him.

"Now that's what I am talking about." Bobbi then turned and walked towards the door. Ben watched her slim body move effortlessly. Sarah may teach sports, but Bobbi actually played them, and not too long ago either—lettering in soccer as well as tennis in high school and playing intramurals all through college. Her long strawberry-blonde hair, free from pony-tails or braids, bounced invitingly behind her, calling him.

Ben looked down at his shoes. Perhaps Phil was also right about him and Bobbi. Perhaps he was somehow leading her on, leaning on her as his "work spouse," and in so doing encouraging feelings that they both should not be feeling. Perhaps the continual phone calls, a necessary part of the job—or so he thought—were actually creating a bond that spilled over into other areas of their lives, complicating things.

It was Bobbi, after all, whom Ben called first when he flew into a new city or checked into a new hotel. Supposedly he would call her to check on the situation at the office or find out if there was anything new he needed to know at the last minute before seeing a client or attending a meeting, but they always seemed to talk longer than he had expected and discussed topics he had no intention of discussing—especially later on, after the meeting, when he was bored or lonely or depressed, and he'd call her again, just to report.

And then they would talk about things not even remotely connected to work, too—college, cars, growing up in Michigan, early dating experiences, tennis, hopes for the future, even his kids, even Sarah. Ben felt a cloud of shame creep over his previously sunny mood. He had to do something about this. He just did not know what.

Before she left the room, Bobbi turned again towards him. "Oh, I forgot to tell you that I called the number you left me, and the guy came and picked up your car."

Ben was floored. All thoughts of his relationship with Bobbi were instantly blown out of his brain. "My Lexus?"

Bobbi smiled. "Not to worry, the place checked out," she said, matter-of-factly, pausing playfully between each sentence, toying with him. "It is a body shop in Anderson. ... It's run by some guy named Billy, just Billy. ... He came highly recommended on all the Internet sites. ... He knew everything about your accident and said that it would be ready in a week. ... He even has a paint and body shop on site so he can do everything there. ... When he showed up, I gave him the spare key you had in your desk and made him sign a receipt just in case. You never know, you know."

She slowly began to back out of the room, seemingly waiting for his reaction.

Ben did not know how to react. "So my Lexus is gone?" he said.

"That's right. Billy came about half an hour ago. He was a very nice man. Very respectful and polite—although he does have a problem with swearing."

"So, I have no car?" Ben's brain was still in neutral, running but completely unengaged.

By this time, Bobbi was almost out of the room. She started to close the door and then stopped, with only her head visible. "Oh, did I forget to mention that someone else sent a rental over for you at about the same time?"

Ben still could not get his mind in gear. Bobbi's words bounced off of him like so much rain. "So the Lexus is somewhere in Anderson? And I have another car?"

"Yep. Free of charge."

At this point, Ben's mind clicked into gear. "What kind?"

Ben could only see Bobbi's lips by this point. The door was almost completely shut. "I haven't seen it myself, but the agreement seemed to indicate that it was a ... Hyundai."

"A Hyundai!" Ben yelled, grabbed his laptop and bounded across the room. Bobbi flung the door wide open and stepped aside, just in time. Ben was almost instantly out the door, down the hall, and outside before she could even blink—all the while muttering words like "parsimonious," "avaricious," "rapacious," "money-grubbing," "rinky-dink," in connection with "insurance companies." Ben's English-major vocabulary blossomed when he was angry.

But it all stopped as soon as he saw the most beautiful car he had even seen parked directly in front of him—a brand-new metallic green Equus.

Sorry, I Have to Take This

Late Again

> *For many business professionals, electronic involvement represents a continual temptation. It is much easier to compose an e-mail, text a colleague, or check Facebook than to do strategic items such as writing a brief, creating a presentation, setting up a meeting to reward or terminate an employee, or dealing with a complex billing situation. Electronic activities not only are generally smaller and simpler but they also provide almost instant feedback and allow persons to explore their curiosity—usually, though, without much being accomplished.*

    Ben did not know what to say—or what to do. He was overwhelmed. He did not know that rental companies even owned cars like this, much less let them out as "loaners." He walked slowly beside the Equus, running his hand gently along its flawless surface, his fingers tingling at the touch. It was real. It was not a hallucination, something concocted from a brain obsessed since childhood with cars.
    He placed both of his hands on the hood, like he was blessing it and could somehow feel, deep in his body, the power of its 5.0L 429-horsepower V8 engine, the smoothness of its specially designed 8-speed SHIFTRONIC automatic transmission, and the stability made possible by a sport-tuned suspension system. In an almost visceral way, he understood instantly the grace with which it handled corners and the speed of its nearly instant acceleration.
    Bobbi, now beside him, explained everything about the rental agreement—its details, and time limits, and conditions—but Ben only heard scattered phrases—"Fleischmann Fund," "fully insured," "unlimited mileage,"

"Bluetooth connection." He was too busy reverencing this marvel of modern engineering. He tried the driver's side door. It opened easily and he got in. The aroma of new leather overwhelmed his senses as did the sight of the polished mahogany trim and the immaculate interior. Ben sank deep into the ergodynamically-designed seat.

Bobbi handed Ben the key fob. He took it without thinking and pressed the large start button. Instantly the Equus came alive, the automatic steering wheel moving quietly into place and an 8-inch display screen lighting up—revealing in vivid graphics the temperature outside as well as that of the driver's side and the passenger's side. An adjacent touchscreen indicated that more information—the current height of the vehicle, the condition of its suspension, and other systems—was also available to him—as were GPS directions, music controls, and detailed trip information on other displays. It was as though he had been transported in time, forward to an era much more technologically advanced than his, a time where everything was well ordered and waiting eagerly for his command.

Still, it was hard for him to stay excited about the Equus. After all, he had just been in a meeting where the limitations of technology had been vividly shown to him. As Phil would say, this car for all of its advanced engineering and high-tech gadgetry was just another "pretty toy" created to distract him from "more important things." In the end, it was just another gas-powered engine mounted on four wheels, guided by a steering wheel, and kept in check with a brake. All the computerized sensors and digital safety devices and video monitors in the world would not have kept him from hitting Phil's rusty truck, not today anyway. They had limitations—and drawbacks—and costs—things salespeople rarely talk about. The touchscreen flickered.

And then there was Bobbi, standing just outside his window, grinning at him, so pleased, so happy that she could make him happy—seemingly waiting expectantly for him to reciprocate somehow, to reinforce his bond with her just as she had just reaffirmed her bond to him. She was like an emotional vacuum cleaner, sucking the joy out of the Equus just as she had ruined his positive feelings after the meeting.

Ben pushed the start button again and got out. "It will do," he said and then promptly marched back to his office. He was already seated in front of his laptop, opening a new Word document, when Bobbi again caught up with him.

"Ben," she said, using his given name for the first time—at least the first time he could recall. "Is there something wrong? Aren't you pleased? That is a $45,000 car out there. When the rental company called and asked what kind of car you wanted, I told them to send the best they had and this is it—an Equus, the highest ranked large premium car for customer appeal." Bobbi had obviously done some research.

She paused, gathering her thoughts, and then continued. "I thought I'd never get you out of that car. I thought you'd already be on I-71, trying it out. I mean, it is nearly four anyway—not much time left to really do anything anyway."

Ben checked the clock on his computer. Four already? Where did the day go? He cleared his throat. "I am pleased with the car, Bobbi," he said still looking at the computer screen. "I really am. It's just that I need to get a few things done first before I go home—to my wife and kids. That's all."

The words sounded flat, even to Ben. He said the words automatically, almost without thinking—he was just trying to get rid of her—but as he heard them come out of his mouth, he realized just how true they were. He really did *need* to get something done. He *needed* to accomplish something, everything, anything. This afternoon's meeting had reminded him what being focused felt like, and he wanted that feeling back. He did not like the way his mind seemed to be wandering lately, always moving from one thing to another, scattered.

"Oh, okay," Bobbi responded, still sounding somewhat confused but unwilling to push the issue further. "I think I understand. You're feeling pressured again, right? You're still worried about meeting this quarter's goals. Well, let me just say again that I think you've come up with a brilliant strategy, and if anyone can implement it well, you can. I have faith in you, and in the department. You'll make it. I'm sure of it."

"Thanks, Bobbi," Ben said, again without looking at her. All this praise coming from her made him uncomfortable. He just wanted Bobbi to leave. After a few seconds, she did so, almost sneaking out, tiptoeing on her pumps, barely making a sound. Only the click of the latch told Ben that she had finally left the room and he was alone—at last.

Ben let out a sigh of relief. "Okay," he said to himself, "I have an hour before I need to leave for Aaron's soccer game. What I need now is one really good idea."

He stared at the blank Word document for several seconds. But nothing came. He tried summoning up the meeting in his mind, concentrating on what the reps had said, searching for something he could do to help—maybe answer a question, provide some hint, some encouragement with a particularly difficult task, spur them on somehow. Nothing.

He tried thinking about his experience as a rep and the way he had been trained—trying to find some nugget, some pithy saying he could send them or program to suggest to help. Again nothing. It was as though his mind was as blank as the digitized page in front of him. This was hard.

Ben looked at the clock on his computer. It was 4:10. Time was dribbling out, leaking away. He launched his e-mail service, hoping that perhaps something there would give him an idea. Nope, just a message from John complimenting him on running such a great meeting and another from Radhika asking him how to fill out an expense report. Ben quickly thanked John and dashed off an answer to Radhika. He even took a few seconds to look up the expense form on the company web site and include its URL in his response to her. He told her to call Bobbi if she had any other questions about the form.

While he was writing to Radhika, two more e-mails from corporate HR appeared, each with "Urgent: personnel change" in the subject. Ben opened them and learned that Walter Hickle, a VP over the California/Silicon region, had been replaced by Madeline Gomez and that all correspondence to that department should go through Max Singh, Madeline's admin. Ben passed on both notes to his department—it only took a moment—and thanked them again for an extraordinary meeting—with, of course, a few jokes at Sid's expense. He also reminded them that he would need this week's numbers a day early this week since Bobbi was taking Friday off.

Ben also thought about sending Madeline a note of congratulations on her promotion and asking her for any ideas she had, but he decided against it. Madeline was a long-time friend for sure, but she was also a competitor now. He did not want to give her any false sense of superiority and, besides, he wanted his department's effort to be just their own.

He therefore simply congratulated her on her promotion over the "second best" sales group in the company. Ben knew she would get a kick out of that. The California group had been number one in sales for nearly three years. Out of curiosity, Ben checked the preliminary sales numbers from the last quarter. Yep, Madeline's department was still number one. It was going to be very hard to displace them. Not even Northeast/New England, the region in second, was close.

About this time Ben heard a tiny knock on his door.

"Yes?" he sighed, keeping his eyes fixed on his computer.

The door creaked. "Sorry to bother you, Boss," Bobbi's voice whispered. "But I forgot to tell you that I went over to the Apple store at the mall while you were having your meeting and bought you the latest iPhone."

61

"Oh thanks, Bobbi," Ben said absently. "That was really nice of you." Ben continued to work on his Word document and typed out "Good ideas" at the top to help get himself started—or to at least look like he was getting started.

"Like I said, I thought you would want to take out the Equus for a test drive right after the meeting so I left the iPhone there, in the storage compartment between the front seats."

"Good." Ben typed out "Idea Number 1."

"It's all ready to go. It has the same number as your old cell, and I keyed in most of the numbers you usually use. The sales guy also said it could be connected, somehow, to the Equus, but I don't remember how he said to do it. Sorry."

"That's all right, Bobbi. Thanks for doing all that for me. You've been a big help."

Bobbi did not say anything more. Ben expected her to leave, but she did not. Even without looking up, he could tell she was still standing in the doorway. Finally, he looked up. He was surprised to see her dressed in her brown leather jacket, holding a large key ring with "BOBBI" embossed on it in her right hand.

"Is there anything wrong, Bobbi?"

"No, well, yes. I'm sorry if I crossed the line today, in the conference room. You know me; I just get too excited sometimes and forget what I am doing. I don't mean anything by it. Anyway, I hope that I didn't hurt our relationship. I really admire you—as a manager. Not many managers would care as much as you do about their employees, as employees, or listen to them or provide them with so many opportunities to grow. What you did today was really heroic. I can only hope that one day I can be as good of a sales manager as you are. Thank you for being my mentor. I have learned a lot from you."

Ben could not help but notice that Bobbi fiddled with her keys and looked down as she spoke. She looked somehow sad—apologetic even. She seemed to want to talk more—he wanted to talk more—but he just did not have time. He had to come up with some good ideas before five and it was already ... 5:27! Ben stared at his computer clock uncomprehendingly. Where had the time gone?

Ben slammed his laptop shut so hard he made Bobbi jump. He then began searching his office frantically for his computer case. "Thanks, Bobbi," he said as he searched. "I really appreciate what you said and would like to talk to you more about it, but I really have to go. I should have left 25, er 27 minutes ago."

Bobbi joined in the hunt for Ben's lost case and apologized for not reminding him—after all, she knew that he usually had to leave early on Mondays to attend soccer matches. She found the case in the corner, where he had tossed it on his way to the sales meeting, and held it for him as he slipped his laptop into it.

"Thanks, Bobbi. I don't know what I would do without you," Ben said quickly, and without thinking, out of reflex more than anything, patted her supportively on the arm. And then he was out the door and into the Equus. In a few seconds, he was on his way.

Sorry, I Have to Take This

Driving Home

As they attempt to focus, business professionals must realize that they need to complete strategic items in the first half of the day. This is because there are typically fewer uncertainties in the first rather than in the second half of the day. Also, most professionals generally have more energy in the earlier parts of the day. Therefore, it's a good idea to create a specific time early in the day when you are not available. This time zone allows you to get away from everything and use that time for creative enterprises—to do serious thinking with no distractions. It should be formally scheduled so that coworkers and clients recognize and respect this time.

Ben was already on Montgomery Road, speeding toward I-71 and home, when it dawned on him what he had just done. "'I don't know what I would do without you,'" he repeated out loud, smacking himself in the head. "What was I thinking?" And stroking her arm? That was practically an invitation for an affair, an admission that his marriage was in trouble and that he was looking for something else—someone else. Ben pulled into a bank parking lot on the right and started looking for his new cell phone. He found it just where Bobbi had told him it would be and dialed Sarah's cell. It rang several times and then Sarah's voice came on the line, requesting that he leave a short message.

"Sarah, this is Ben. I am so sorry. I got tied up at work again. I know, I know. I am sorry. I was all set to leave at five and then I … uh … got some e-mails I needed to answer. Anyway, I will be at the game as quickly as I can.

It's at the fields off Buckwheat, right? Near the high school? Okay, I love you and ..."

"Ben?"

"Sarah? Listen, I'm sorry I'm late. Did you hear my message?"

"Yes. The match was postponed until tomorrow. The camp director thought they needed one more day to hone their skills before showing them off." Ben felt a wave of relief wash over him.

"But you will be back soon, won't you?" she continued. "I have that special PE faculty meeting I told you about tonight. We were going to finalize our plans for this summer's Silly Olympics, and I was counting on you being here to make sure the kids get to bed on time."

"No problem. I'm on my way now. I should be home in about 30 minutes or so."

"No rush. As long as you are home by 6:30. That's when I have to leave for my meeting. Oh, and could you pick up something for the kids to eat? I've got some things to do before I go and I'm running late."

"Sure. I know just the thing." Ben was not really much of a fast food guy, but he loved Cincinnati chili, and he knew the kids liked Coney dogs as well.

"Ben, you are not going to go to Gold Star again, are you?"

"Maybe." Ben was already starting to salivate in anticipation of a plate of Cincinnati chili complete with cheese, onions, red beans, and oyster crackers. He loved five-ways.

"Fine. I don't have time to argue. We're also having a birthday party for one of my colleagues at the meeting and I still have to get my present ready."

A gloom descended upon Ben. He did not have to ask which "colleague" she was talking about. Memories of Derrick leering at Sarah during the last faculty/spouse get-together he attended shot through Ben's mind. Both of them went silent for a moment. Finally Sarah spoke.

"By the way, are you all right? I tried calling you earlier but I couldn't get through."

"You couldn't get through?" Ben puzzled over her words and then remembered. "Oh that's right. I had a wreck this morning and broke my cell phone."

"You what?" Sarah screamed, her voice making the cell phone's speaker buzz. "Ben? Are you all right? Is the car all right? Why didn't you call me? Why did you wait until now to tell me?" Sarah's words came out rapid fire, spraying like bullets from a machine gun. Ben winced as each one hit its mark.

He started to explain again that he had broken his cell phone but, fortunately, just before he made a fool of himself, he remembered his land line. Why hadn't he used it? Why hadn't he called Sarah from his office? The phone was right there, all the time, when he was talking to Bobbi. Why hadn't he thought of calling Sarah?

"Sorry," was all he could come up with, and he reassured her that he was fine and that the Lexus would be fine, as soon as it was repaired. He then told her everything about the accident, mostly to distract her and put his stupidity in context. He also emphasized the part Phil played in the success of his meeting and mentioned more than once that Phil was paying for everything. They were not out a single dime.

"Well, I am certainly glad everything worked out so well and that your meeting was a success," Sarah said. "I am also glad you have a rental. I don't know what we would do with just one car, what with our busy schedules and all."

Ben nodded, forgetting that Sarah could not see him.

"So you'll be home before 6:30?" Sarah emphasized again. "Good, because I have to be at the party early to help set up. It's going to be a blast."

"Yes, I will definitely be home before 6:30." Ben's voice sounded robotic, cold and efficient.

"And could you fix the computer too? It still has that virus on it, and I can't access Derrick's site. Every time I try it takes me to a porn site."

"How appropriate," Ben said under his breath.
"What?"
"Nothing, I'll work on it."
"Okay, see you soon. Luv ya."

"Luv ya too." Ben ended the call. He thought about continuing on to I-71 and getting home as quickly as he could, but thought better of it and instead turned left out of the parking lot and went the long way home, through Indian Hill.

After he turned onto Keller and was waiting at the stop sign to go left on Blome, Ben changed his mind about technology for a moment and decided to try out the Equus' 17-speaker sound system. He needed a distraction. Thoreau's "more important things" were getting him down. He tuned into a classical station from the University of Cincinnati. Copland's "Appalachian Spring" was playing. Soon the old Shaker melody, with a full orchestra behind it, filled the Equus' interior, enfolding him in beautiful sound.

Ben was not much of a classical music guy—mostly he liked more popular stuff, songs he'd heard in college—but "Appalachian Spring" was an exception, perhaps because he knew the words. "Tis the gift to be simple; tis the gift to be free," and the words seemed to fit his surroundings. As he pulled onto Blome and later veered right onto Spooky Hollow Road, he found himself surrounded by simple things—an old apple farm on the left and fields with cows in them on the right.

Spooky Hollow had to be his favorite road in all of Cincinnati. Years ago, when he worked for Cyncon, long before DigitALL and Bobbi, he went this way to work every day. He loved the way the trees lined Spooky Hollow on both sides. They seemed to shield him from his problems, their trunks standing like silent sentries with their branches guarding him, protecting him in a glorious canopy of sunlit green.

He did not carry a cell phone with him then. He did not need to, and they were not yet as popular as they are now. In those days, he just drove, without distractions, humming along in his old Subaru, safe between those glorious trees. He thought a lot about things then, on his way to work, and it was odd how he used to have all sorts of ideas just come to him—new ways to sell things, new people he needed to contact, new approaches he could use, as well as new thoughts about the kids and Sarah. He used to treasure those times and for a while continued driving this way even when he went with DigitALL and moved to the new office.

But that was then and this was now. Now he could not afford to go this way every day anymore and he often made calls while he was driving. He needed every second just to stay on schedule—and he was clearly not doing that very well. He sighed as he thought about how miraculous the sales meeting was and how he had wasted so much time that afternoon, time he could have spent helping his reps implement their new strategy. But he got distracted—by e-mails and phone calls and the Internet and fancy rental cars and … Bobbi. He just could not seem to stay focused. He had difficulty staying "on task," as Aaron's teacher said about him. Perhaps he had ADHD as well. Perhaps that is why he was so desperate, as Phil called him.

Ben simply followed Spooky Hollow down its ravine and stopped at the intersection with Loveland-Madeira Road. After looking both ways twice, he turned onto Remington, crossed the Little Miami River and then skirted along its banks. From the road he could see people canoeing on the river's deep green surface, and Ben thought about the canoe trips he and Sarah and the kids had taken along that same river—splashing each other, racing each other, but also just drifting, allowing the current to carry them downstream of its own accord.

Sometimes Sarah and he would put aside their paddles and just float, silently enjoying the sun and the trees and the way the kids seemed to grow before their eyes. Those were not desperate days. They were good days, happy days. Wonderful things just seemed to flow to them, to him back then—work things as well as family things. As long as he kept away from the eddies, avoided the shallows, and made an effort to stay in the current, he made solid progress and enjoyed himself in the process.

Ben smiled as he noticed the fishing poles in the canoes. Occasionally his family would also bring along fishing poles on their trips too, but they would never catch any fish. The kids made too much noise for that to happen. Memories and perspective were the only things they caught back then—well, except for the time a bluegill, surprised by their canoe, drifting silently for once, actually jumped into it when they accidentally brushed against a stand of reeds. The kids still talked about that bluegill and joked that their dad could catch more fish with a canoe than most fathers could with a pole. He would always laugh and explain that the secret was the bait. These fish were suburban fish. They liked potato chips better than they liked worms.

Ben felt a cloud pass over him, darkening his memories, as he approached Miamiville, the scene of his wreck. He slowed down as he drove through the town and nearly stopped at the intersection with Wards-Corner Road before turning into it. He took the corner slowly, all the while being very alert to his surroundings. It all seemed so unreal after everything that had happened today. It seemed almost unthinkable that he could have hit an old codger like Phil. But there Ben was, in a new Hyundai Equus, his wrecked Lexus already in the shop, and off on the right was the sparkle of broken glass as well as the skid marks from Phil's truck.

Yes, the wreck had been real all right. This was no dream. Everything seemed just as he had remembered it from this morning except for one thing. Farther off on the right, almost in the bushes near where Phil had parked, Ben noticed a small sign, low against the ground. It looked like a cross people put up to memorialize their loved ones who had been killed on the highway. Ben pulled over and got out to read it. It was made of weathered wood, imperfectly cut. On it was the Thoreau quotation Phil had recited to him, the one about our inventions being toys that distract us and it had a rough "HDF" carved into it—probably "HDT" at one point but so weathered and poorly done that the letters looked different.

"Yes, I understand cell phones can be hindrances," Ben said, absurdly talking to the sign, as though it was Phil. "They can distract us in meetings and make us less productive. E-mails and the Internet can do that too—as can expensive Korean cars and beautiful administrative assistants. So what do I do about them? I can't very well get rid of them and go live in a cabin alone, like you did. I still have to make a living. I need a way of controlling them, instead of allowing them to control me."

Ben waited for a reply, but none came. He grabbed a fallen branch, probably the same branch that Phil had used to clear the weeds around his sign, and began whacking at the bushes around the sign himself. He was not really sure why he was doing this. It just felt good, almost as though he were attacking something deep in his soul, cutting it down, clearing it out. The tall plants buckled as he hit them and went flying into the bushes. The stickers broke into bunches and collapsed on the ground. And then he saw it—another sign—crude, like the first, wooden, weathered, with similar initials. It read, "Time is but the stream I go a-fishing in. – ADF."

"That's it," Ben practically screamed. He threw his stick into the bushes and began clearing the area around the sign with his hands. Almost immediately they started to bleed from sticker cuts and scrapes from small rocks on the ground. Ben did not care.

He took out his cell phone and took a picture of the now plainly visible sign. Then, finding a pad of paper and a pen, he wrote:

> **Rule 2: Don't take or make any calls while driving to work or for the first hour at the office—no appointments either. Set the time aside to accomplish strategic activities. Ideas will come if you don't drive them away with "noise." They**

are like fish; they take time and patience and quiet to catch.

Rule 2 was much shorter than Rule 1. Later on when he was typing it out on his laptop, he explained that this was his thinking time, a time without distractions—a time when he did not take calls or answer e-mails or hold meetings or have any interactions with anyone at all—including Bobbi. It was his time to just let his mind flow naturally along its course and allow ideas to come to him, just like the bluegill did.

Ben knew that such a policy was expensive—after all, time was money and here he was spending an hour of it, more if he counted his drive to work, on something that was not immediately work-related. But he had to do something and it had worked before. He decided to at least give it a try, a personal experiment for the remainder of the quarter.

He stood up and dusted his pants off. Blood from the cuts on his hands left small streaks on the fabric. It felt like a covenant, a blood promise. "Okay, I solemnly swear to give myself time to think in the mornings even if other things press down on me." Ben high-fived a large mulberry leaf as the final act in his impromptu ritual. Yes, this was going to work. Things were going to change. He turned to go but noticed another piece of wood to his right on the ground in the pile of chopped down weeds. It was one more sign.

He picked it up. It read, "I know of no more encouraging fact than the unquestionable ability of man to elevate his life by conscious endeavor. –WBF."

The initials on this sign were worse, hardly legible. Ben cleaned it off some and placed it upright, leaning against the second. He took a photo of it too with his iPhone. He thanked Phil vicariously and then drove off for home.

Ben was nearly exploding, wanting, needing to tell Sarah about his day. Unfortunately, she was already in the garage, ready to go, waiting for him.

"Thanks for rushing home so quickly," she said as he opened his door, "and for picking up dinner." She looked over the Gold Star bag and shook her head. "I'd lecture you on nutrition but something came up and I have to go right now."

"What? You're leaving? Already?"

Sarah opened the door to her car and got in. "The kids are in the family room," she yelled. "They are watching TV. I'll be back as soon as I can—probably around 11. Don't wait up. Bye." And then she was gone.

Ben watched as Sarah sped off to her party, leaving him alone, with his bag of cheese Coneys to talk to. Ben shrugged his shoulders, grabbed his laptop case, and went inside. Immediately he was mobbed by Amy and Aaron, grabbing for the Coneys. They fairly tore the bag from his hands, ripping open the Styrofoam container, and stuffing the hotdogs garnished with mustard, chili, onions, and cheese into their eager mouths. They were starving. This was late for them to eat.

Ben pulled up a chair beside them and tried to engage them in a conversation about fishing and canoeing, but they ate too quickly and soon left him alone, twirling the spaghetti of his five-way chili on his fork.

After dinner, Ben found his kids in front of the TV and sent them off to their rooms to get ready for bed. After he made sure that they had actually obeyed him, he went into the den, fired up the family computer and started scanning it again for viruses. While he waited he opened up his laptop and transferred his second rule to it, elaborating on it and explaining it in greater detail.

This got Ben thinking about Phil again and, once the scan was complete and the virus was once again quarantined, he googled "Phil Fleischmann," "the Fleischman fund," "Fleischmann yeast," and just plain "Fleischmann." He was certain that there was some connection between Phil and the legendary family of the same name, and he felt that if there were, there was a good chance he could turn it to his economic advantage—perhaps as an "in" to some large corporation that desperately needed more data storage devices or some other product DigitALL sold. However, try as he might he could not find a connection.

He learned a great deal about Charles and Maximilian Fleischmann—their Moravian roots, their background in yeast making, their incredible success in business as well as the amazing home Charles's grandson Julius II, the son of Julius, had built in Indian Hill, not very far from Ben's work—but nothing about Phil or some other truck-driving, Thoreau-spouting Fleischmann kid who had for some reason gone "granola" and started a one-man campaign against cell phones.

Ben also checked Facebook to see if Phil had a page there. However, something Sarah sent out from her page, which appeared on his, distracted him, and he spent the next hour scrutinizing her page and then Derrick's page for clues as to how far their relationship had gone. In the end, he still was not sure. However, what he saw was not comforting. Derrick had added several folders of new photos—mostly pictures of himself demonstrating new exercises. He was always portrayed shirtless, pumped up, greased and grinning stupidly at the camera, or, more likely, at Sarah behind the camera. Ben saw her left hand in one of the photos, tense, gripping a piece of equipment supposedly to balance herself. She was not wearing her wedding ring. Ben logged out. He had to do something about this.

The Next Day

> *Admittedly setting aside a time for personal planning may seem counterproductive to colleagues and others who require one's attention. However, if implemented consistently and compassionately, such an approach will eventually yield results that will be obvious to most. They will come to understand that your having a secluded time zone is in their best interests.*

The next morning Sarah did not say anything about her party, and Ben did not ask. He basically just went about his business—getting dressed, eating breakfast, and making sure he had everything for work: his laptop, his iPhone, his watch, his socks, the usual. He then made sure the kids were up and had plenty of cereal to eat—his job—and then he was off, zipping around I-275, doing his best not to think about Sarah and Derrick and their party. Far from intruding, the Equus' distractions were welcome to him now—and helpful. As he played with the onboard Internet display, he discovered that there was a traffic jam on I-71. The site he was looking at even suggested he take Montgomery Road to avoid it. "Take that, Phil," he said out loud. "There is a place for technology in the workplace after all."

Just then a ring tone went off, some unknown ditty Bobbi had programmed into his iPhone, and Ben began fumbling for his phone. However, remembering his resolution and fearing that he might be tempting fate by answering it, he changed his mind and decided to let it ring. Technology had done its job. Now it was time for him to do his. Now was his time to think.

The problem with thinking for Ben was that he had not done it for a long time—not so much thinking per se, but thinking creatively, imaginatively, and especially doing so over an extended period.

He was out of the habit. Ben felt fidgety as he drove and found his attention wandering—jumping from business matters to cars to the weather to Sarah to Derrick and finally to Bobbi.

How was Bobbi going to react when he told her he did not want any contact with her for the first 60 minutes of work every morning? Surely she would not understand. That had been their time. Bobbi often brought bagels or pastries into his office and ate them with him as they went over his schedule for the day. Ben could tell that she valued this time and loved surprising him with new delights. It was an important ritual for her. She was not going to be pleased with this change.

And yet it had to be made. Not only did Ben need the time to think, but he needed more distance from Bobbi. They were becoming too close, too dependent upon one another—too much like Sarah and Derrick. Ben noticed a billboard on his left advertising the opening of a local gym. A well-built, and well-oiled, shirtless man was helping a young woman pump iron. She was wearing almost as little as he was and was smiling adoringly at the oily man. Yes, a change had to be made. He had to focus more.

And so, exercising all of his will power, Ben attempted to first think of his reps, visualizing them making calls and concentrating on what they needed to keep the new departmental initiative going. But just as had happened the day before, he could not think of any new ideas. Despite his best efforts, his attention kept bouncing back to Sarah and Derrick pumping iron together, maybe even making billboards together. "If only Derrick had more experience in business," he told himself. "If only he had former clients, like my reps had, and knew whom to contact and how, then perhaps he would be busier and would not have to rely so much on Sarah and this stupid video idea." The problem was that Derrick just didn't know who his customers were or how to reach them.

The Next Day

Something suddenly clicked inside Ben's head. Yes, some of his reps were a lot like Derrick. They were so new and so inexperienced that they too did not know whom to contact or how to approach them. Therefore, they spun their wheels a lot, going nowhere fast, getting frustrated. If he could put together a list of former DigitALL customers for them and add just a few hints as to how to approach them, they would at least know where to begin and would eventually be much more successful much more quickly.

Suddenly the mental pace of Ben's trip quickened and he ceased noticing the cars and road signs along the way. His mind raced as he thought of all the former customers he knew or had heard about, and he considered what advice he might give his reps about them. Seemingly he arrived at the DigitALL building in no time, and he sprinted out of the Equus and up to his office. Bobbi looked startled to see him appear so suddenly and so quickly, almost out of nowhere. Ben noticed she had some luscious-looking schnecken from Busken's on her desk. He thought about grabbing one as he passed her, but there was no time. He had work to do.

"Sorry, Bobbi," Ben said breathlessly. "I just thought of something, and I have to write it down before I forget it." He then went into his office and shut the door before she could say anything. He whipped out his laptop and began typing. He did not bother to organize the customers into areas or to regularize his thoughts. He simply wrote his thoughts down as quickly as he could, noting anything that came to his mind: names, titles, positions, history, quirks, needs, concerns, even rumors.

Some of the information was most certainly out-of-date and some might have never been true. Nonetheless, some information was better than none, and knowing what was said about these people in the hallways and at the water coolers of DigitALL might help his reps. And so Ben wrote on, feeling that at least what he had to say made these customers seem more like real people and less like faceless bureaucrats.

However, when Ben finished his "free writing," he realized he needed to at least check a few of his "facts" to make sure he was not totally off base and, although it was technically against the spirit of Rule 2, Ben went to the Internet and began looking up some of these companies' websites. He was amazed at how much information was available to him—not just addresses and phone numbers but, if he knew where to look, contacts, job titles, even product needs, and, occasionally, product evaluations. Continuing with the theme of his morning commute, he was discovering that technology was not all bad. In fact it was indispensable if it was used correctly. The question was how to use it correctly so that it did not distract him from "serious things."

But Ben decided to think about that later. Right now he was starting to feel hungry. He looked at his watch. It was after nine. "Wow," he said to himself. "Time really flies when your mind is engaged." He instantly thought of several things he still needed to do that day, but he did not feel badly about not yet getting to them. Mostly he just felt hungry. After all, this had been an incredibly productive hour and a half, as far as he could see. However, he did feel guilty about leaving Bobbi in the lurch so long without an explanation.

Ben opened his door cautiously and peaked out. No Bobbi. And no schnecken either. Ben walked into her office and looked down the hallway. There was no sign of her. He walked down to the break room, hoping to see her or at least a schnecken, but she was not there and the schnecken box sat empty, except for a few crumbs, on the counter near the microwave. Ben plunked in a few coins into the vending machine and bought a hermetically-sealed pastry and attempted to eat it. It was nothing like a schnecken, and he threw half of it in the waste basket. He then went back to his office, all the time keeping an eye out for Bobbi.

He thought about searching for her—checking out the printer room and all the other places she might be—but decided against it. He did not want to give the impression he

The Next Day

was seeking her out for non-business purposes, and he decided that perhaps telling her about the change impersonally through a general e-mail to the entire department would be better. After all, he did not want Bobbi to think he was doing this just because of her. If she heard about it the same way and time everyone else did, she would surely know that this was just a business decision with no personal component—although there was one.

And so Ben drafted a short e-mail briefly announcing his new "private time" and explaining how he wanted to be free to think without interruptions or distractions from 8 to 9. He would use this time to come up with new business approaches and strategies and therefore would not be taking calls or holding meetings of any kind during his first hour of work. Finally, hoping to end on an inspiring note, Ben added that this was an exciting and important time for DigitALL and for the Midwest region, and he hoped that everyone would see the benefit of this policy at this time.

Ben looked over his work. He liked it—concise, to the point, upbeat, business-like, and clear. He liked clarity. He then sent it out to his entire department and began working his way through the 20-plus new e-mails that had already appeared since yesterday. He got through about two before he decided to send Bobbi another e-mail. He just could not let go of his list idea. It needed more work, but obviously he could not work on it now. He therefore asked her to go through the departmental records and make a list of all the former DigitALL customers for the last five years, complete with contact information if possible, arranged by area. He attached the file he had started and explained that this was the kind of information he was looking for. He then went back to dealing with his e-mails, which had increased by five just in the time it took him to compose a note to Bobbi.

It was lunch by the time he had finished. Some phone calls and a long discussion with Bill about incentive pay slowed his effort. Ben left his office and looked again for Bobbi but she was still nowhere to be seen. However, on her desk, in a company folder, was the report he had asked for.

Ben sighed. All he had wanted was a draft, something like the draft he had sent her, to which he could add more comments. He had not wanted her to spend her entire morning polishing the thing. He knew she had other, more pressing, things to do. He just wanted the raw data so he could build upon it and polish it out later. But Bobbi, being the perfectionist she was, had created a publishable book, impeccably formatted, complete with footnotes and time stamps. She had even numbered the pages and added "DigitALL Confidential" in the header. Oh well, he thought, I don't want to offend her. I'll just add my stuff in the margins and have her send it out as is.

And so Ben took Bobbi's manuscript to lunch with him and worked on it while he had a sandwich at the Kenwood Towne Center food court. He was surprised at the number of ideas that came into his head once he got started. He had not really been in this job a long time, but he had had lots of face-to-face experience with these people—or else he had somehow heard a lot about them. His notes practically filled all the margins and leaked into the spaces between lines. There was so much to say. After all, sales was an art, and he had been quite good at it once. After he had finished his comments, he then picked up some shirts that were on sale at Lazarus and bought a belt to go with his new black shoes. All in all, it took him about an hour and he was back in the office, wearing his new belt. By then Bobbi was back as well.

"Hi Bobbi," he said cheerfully. His productive lunch left him feeling energetic as did his new belt. He noticed that Bobbi was also wearing an outfit he was 87% sure was new—a summery green and blue ensemble with a gypsy-like scarf around her waist. She looked stunning. He thought about complimenting her, but decided against it in case he was wrong or she decided to take what he said in a wrong way.

The Next Day

"Nice job on the list of former customers," he said instead, sticking to business. "Thank you for putting it together so quickly and so well."

"You are most welcome," she said, without looking up at him or stopping her typing.

"I added a few more comments to it," Ben continued. "Would you please divide it up according to area and send the separate parts out to the reps for me?"

"Today?" Bobbi stopped typing. She seemed surprised.

"Yes, if that's possible."

"Yes, sir," Bobbi responded flatly and resumed her typing. She did not say anything else. She simply nodded to a place on her desk to put the manuscript.

To his knowledge, Bobbi had never "sirred" him before. He stood there, motionless beside her desk, scrutinizing the top of her head, searching for some clue as to what was going on inside it. Something was wrong. He was sure of it.

"Bobbi?" he began, moving closer to her desk. But just then his cell phone rang. He looked at the display. It was Sarah. "Sorry, I need to take this," he said and reentered his office.

"Sarah? Is anything wrong?" Sarah almost never called him in the early afternoon.

"Hi Ben, no nothing's wrong. I'm just calling to remind you about Aaron's soccer match this evening. Remember? It was switched from yesterday. I just thought it might not be on your calendar. I know it may not seem like much—a match in the middle of soccer camp—but it's a big deal for a lot of kids, a chance to demonstrate their new skills and show off."

"I remembered."

"I knew you would. And I also wanted to ask you to pick up some treats for after the game—you know, just some juice boxes and cookies or something. It's our turn and I have another PE faculty meeting this afternoon so I can't get them."

"I thought you had a faculty meeting last night? School is not even in session. What do you all have to talk about?" Ben could not keep an accusative tone out of his voice.

Sarah laughed. "Last night? Oh that was crazy. Derrick somehow found out that we had planned a surprise birthday for him and put together a surprise of his own. I'll tell you all about it when you get home."

"Yeah, I bet you will."

Sarah went silent for a moment. "Ben, what are you saying? Nothing is going on. Derrick and I are just colleagues, co-workers, nothing more. It's kind of like you and Bobbi."

Ben winced. He looked out of his office door and saw Bobbi looking at him. He walked over and shut the door before saying anything else.

"It's nothing like Bobbi and me," he said, almost whispering. "We don't come to work in skimpy exercise outfits and take pictures of each other getting all sweaty." He thought again about the two people in the gym billboard.

"I don't know. Maybe you do. I don't know what you do at work!" Sarah voice was getting louder as Ben's softened. "You never talk about it. For all I know, you do do those things."

Ben felt his jaw tighten. "I try to talk to you, but you are always gone. Like last night. I wanted to tell you all about this fantastic meeting I had, but you took off to party with Derrick."

"That was one night in three months. You're the one who is always gone to meetings."

"I am not. I have not been to a single meeting at night in a year."

"Well, you have been on the phone. It's the same thing. You're out of touch for hours."

"It's not the same thing," Ben said, but part of him wondered if she was right. He thought again about his meeting yesterday.

Sarah sighed. "Look, we're not going to solve this now. Let's talk about this when you get home—after Aaron's game. In the meantime, please pick up the treats this time, okay?"

"Okay," Ben agreed and almost instantly forgot what he had just agreed to do.

"Well, bye then."

"Bye."

Ben sat down at his desk and stared out the window. The sugar maple across the parking lot, the one beside the pool in an apartment complex next door, was still radiant in its new summer green, the sun filtering through its leaves, but would not be long before its leaves would start to turn, starting with ones at the top and then moving down gradually like colored icing—or blood. Time was marching on, and he was not prepared.

Ben spent the rest of the day filling out reports and attending, via conference call, a managers-only HR meeting. The meeting was so dull and so long that he purposely broke his Rule 1 and began surfing the Internet after about ten minutes. He started off by looking up websites of some other former customers he remembered, thinking that it might be good to double-check Bobbi's work and issue an addendum if need be.

However, Derrick was still on Ben's mind, and so eventually, after about four or five customers, he left off researching companies and turned his attention to Derrick, searching for clues concerning his relationship with Sarah. However, he didn't find any. Derrick now had a website, "Building Bulk with Derrick," and an official Facebook page promoting his business. It was slicker than his personal page and showed only the best of the photos Sarah had taken. Ben scrutinized them again looking for what really motivated the man. However, there was nothing "internal" in these photos—no expressions of feelings or thoughts or hopes or dreams, just picture after picture of a well-built body working out. For all the world, Derrick seemed to Ben to be a complete dough-head. He had no idea why Sarah—cultured, sensitive, intelligent Sarah—would be attracted to a guy like him.

Was that how Bobbi looked to Sarah? Since he was already in Facebook, Ben decided to find out. He looked up her page and saw the complete opposite of Derrick's. Sure, there were photos on her page— photos of vacations she had taken to Mackinaw Island, Chicago, Mammoth Cave, Nashville, and Whitewater River in Indiana—but she was never alone in them and always fully clothed. And the photos, as good as they were, were not the focus of the page. Her page was full of information about herself—how she studied business at Miami of Ohio, graduated in three years, lived in Mariemont, was unmarried, no kids, and liked the Cincinnati Symphony almost as much as she liked the outdoors. Her site was full of reviews of local events and opinions about movies and plays and books. Ben was overwhelmed, and more than a little disappointed that never once was her handsome boss mentioned—or her work. In fact, she seemed to have bigger plans that that, something along the lines of becoming an executive or owning her own business.

The meeting lasted an hour, but it had been over nearly half an hour before Ben noticed. The phone never buzzed or clicked or made any sound whatsoever. It simply went dead and Ben, who had already mentally hung up, did not notice the change. To him it had become just white noise, something to hear but not listen to.

He hung up and checked his e-mail again. Mr. Shaw had sent out a follow-up note congratulating the presenters and telling everyone how excited he was about this new direction the company was taking—so excited that he was going to "test" his VPs' knowledge during his next set of interviews. Ben started to panic. He realized he had not heard a thing and knew nothing about any "new direction." However, mercifully Mr. Shaw added that he would soon be sending out the speakers' slides as well as a transcript of the meeting to everyone later on. Ben sighed and looked at his watch. It was 5:30. He quickly closed his laptop. He was late again.

At the Soccer Field

The problem of electronic distraction is not limited just to business. It is also apparent in other areas, and if it is not carefully monitored, technology can distract us from our core activities at home as well as in the office. It's easy to blur the lines between professional and personal activities. You may start out working and end up surfing the Internet, or you may simply be checking your messages with the family and end up talking to a colleague for an hour during an important family event. Such infringement leaves both parties feeling short-changed.

Ben raced out of his office almost as quickly as he had raced into it that morning. Bobbi was still there, typing away on something. "Late," "soccer game," "dead," and "talk tomorrow" were about the only sounds Ben managed to utter that even remotely resembled words as he rushed by Bobbi's desk. Then he was gone.

Hoping that the GPS in the Equus knew of some secret, extra fast way to the Finley Ray Soccer Fields in Milford, Ben checked it for directions. No luck. I-71 to I-275 and then into Finley Ray using the Milford Parkway was the best it could come up with. Ben pushed the Equus as fast as he dared go, weaving in an out of traffic, all the way to the park. He had left the GPS on and he made it a personal goal to beat its estimated times before exits and turn offs. Ben arrived, feeling like he had won a race, a feeling curiously similar to the one he felt this morning when he had arrived at work ready with his new idea.

However, getting to the fields was not even half the battle. Ben still had to find Aaron's group and a place to park This was not going to be easy. The exhibition matches were the highlight of soccer camp. Hordes of campers in brightly colored shirts, most with their names on them, were scattered throughout the fields, some running, most standing around, looking lost—their parents and other visitors sitting in folding chairs or standing stoically on the sidelines.

It was a mess. Cars were parked everywhere, not just in crude parking lots but along the fields and beside the roads. Occasionally Ben would hear the dull thump of a mis-kicked ball striking the hood or side of a car. He would flinch each time. The very idea of that happening to a car like his Equus made him physically ill.

After about 15 more minutes, Ben found a spot on the other side of the fields, near a picnic shelter and, through sheer luck, happened upon the field where Aaron was playing. The teams were huddled around their coaches. For a moment Ben thought he had somehow made it in time. Sarah, however, quickly corrected him.

"Thought you'd take in the last quarter, did you?"

"Last quarter?" Ben's confident smile disappeared. "Aren't they just starting?"

"No," Sarah practically spat. "The match started forty-five minutes ago. Aaron's team is behind 0 to 2."

"Well, I'm just in time for the comeback," Ben said, trying to put a good face on things. Sarah wasn't buying it.

"So what happened?"

"With what?"

Sarah glared at him, forgetting that the match was about to resume. "What do you mean, 'With what?' With you. With you supporting your son. It is enough that you don't care about me, but this is your son. What has happened to you, Ben? I see you forgot the snacks as well."

The snacks! Ben opened his mouth to explain, but nothing came out. He had no idea how he could have been so stupid. He looked around. Several other parents, mostly mothers, were staring at him.

"Could we talk about this some other time, Sarah?" he said, covering his mouth with his hand.

At the Soccer Field

"Sure, why not?" Sarah said even more loudly. "We put everything else off for another time. Why not this? What does a kid's soccer match mean anyway? It's not as if he is going to make money off of it or anything."

"Sarah?" Ben pleaded. And she stopped talking, for the moment. She just stood there, arms crossed, her face turned steadfastly towards the field but not really noticing that both teams had retaken the field and were now about to kick off.

"I implemented a new policy at work today," Ben said, trying to lessen the tension.

"Is that so?" Sarah said without emotion, gazing off toward the fields, not really looking at them. "Did you fix the computer?"

"Yes."

"Good." And after a few minutes of silence she finally asked him about his new policy, blandly stating that it probably made lots of "things" happen.

"Actually, it was and it did," Ben added and then explained to her how he had started a cell-phone-free hour in his day and how he had thought up the idea of sending a list of former customers to his reps.

Sarah just stared at him, her mouth tightening and her face reddening. Ben could see that she was upset about something, and he was about to ask her about it, but before she could respond her phone rang. The melody from Olivia Newton-John's song "Let's Get Physical" filled the air around them. Sarah continued to stare at him as she pulled her cell out of her purse and then turned to see who was calling. Her expression changed completely. Suddenly she was smiling and words came easily to her.

"Oh, I just got a text from Derrick. He probably wants to talk about our session tomorrow. I have to take this." And then Sarah walked away from the field to a spot back towards the trees to text him—as if texting required a quiet place.

Now it was Ben's turn to stare at the field without really seeing anything. Derrick again? Couldn't that guy leave Sarah alone? Ben had never really liked Derrick, but now that he had seen his Facebook page, he was disgusted. "Piece of mindless meat," he said under his breath.

What did Sarah see in him? He had the IQ of a horsefly and a smell to match. Every time he came over to the house to "train" Sarah or to work on their video, the place reeked of sweat. Ben never had liked the idea of her working with him. He understood her need to work and to connect with people outside of their home. But why him? Instead of helping him set up his business, she could be setting up her own. She had as many credentials. She was just a competent and qualified. He especially did not see why he had to train her and why at their home. Everything about this seemed wrong.

But thinking like this was not getting Ben anywhere. He was just getting angry. He had to think of something else. Since he was there, he decided to actually watch the game he had come to see and discovered that Aaron was playing goal keeper. Ben felt sick again. Not goal keeper. He had tried Aaron in goal when they were kicking the ball around in the yard. Ben set up cones for goals and let Aaron shoot at him. But Aaron wanted to try goal keeping himself and he was not too bad at it—as long as someone was shooting on him again and again. But if they were not, Aaron was walking around the goal, picking up clovers, investigating bugs, knocking the cones on their sides and seeing if he could balance them on their points. Aaron had great reflexes and could block an amazing number of balls well, but he had the attention span of a flea. This was a recipe for disaster.

However, this time Aaron seemed to be alert and concentrating. Ben studied the field and then noticed something interesting. The coach had assigned one of his assistants to talk to Aaron. The guy was situated down at the end of the coach's box, as close to Aaron as the rules allowed, and he was telling him, in a steady stream of words, everything that was going on down at the other end of the field, helping him remember what he was doing so that when the ball came his way, Aaron was prepared and focused. It was brilliant and Aaron did not miss a single shot attempted on him. In a way, he was one of the heroes of the day. His team won 3-2, in a dramatic, come-from-behind victory.

Instantly Ben saw a connection to his work on the Internet today. He too could accomplish a lot as long as he had a stated and clear purpose, as when he was looking for customer information. However, when he was just using the Internet, and particularly Facebook, to ease his boredom, without any particular aim in mind, he got all tangled up in himself, just like Aaron did in the net once when Ben had left him alone to play goal keeper. He lost focus and, in a sense, lost the game.

Ben pulled out his iPhone and began texting himself:

Rule 3: Always have a specific purpose and a time period in mind when using the Internet, especially social networking sites. Write it down and stick to it. If you can, even set an alarm to remind you.

Sure, the rule seemed a little strict, but Ben could remember other instances when he had "surfed" away an afternoon—once even when he was under a tight deadline to get a report out. He had known he had to finish the report and yet still had spent hours looking for just the right sound system for his Lexus and then for his house and then for his morning run. The time had seemed to evaporate, and he had paid the price.

If coming up with good ideas was like fishing on a quiet river, then using the Internet was like splashing about, paddling from feeder creek to feeder creek. Obviously the creeks were full of interesting bugs and minnows and frogs and such, but going after them scared away the big fish and never allowed you to get anywhere. The Internet could be incredibly helpful at times, but it also contained a lot of irrelevant and distracting information, information which often still had to be verified. It too, like cell phones, had to be kept in check and Ben, like Aaron, had to be kept focused.

After the game Sarah emerged from the shelter, brushing her hair and smoothing her clothes—almost like she had literally been rolling in the hay instead of figuratively, as Ben suspected. She was surprised, and pleased, that Aaron's team had won. She hugged him and openly berated herself for missing it. However, all the way home Sarah kept checking her cell phone for messages, even while Aaron was recounting his several saves.

Aaron did not seem to notice, but this really irritated Ben—and not just because Sarah was obviously expecting a message from Derrick. He was thinking of Aaron and what that said to him about his mother and her interest in him. When Ben got home he added a new rule to his growing list:

> **Rule 4: Don't check your cell phone or take calls while speaking to someone. Not only is it rude, but also it keeps you from focusing on what that person is saying and limits your response to him or to her. It shows you are not really mentally or emotionally there for the person and indicates you would rather be somewhere else.**

Billy's Garage

However helpful the reduction of negative distractions may be, it is not enough. Successful business professionals must also learn to apply all their liberated mental powers to the task at hand. To do this one must set up boundaries—temporal, even physical boundaries that limit digital distractions and encourage concentration. Along with time zones when one does not answer phones or respond to e-mail or use Facebook, one must arrange one's physical surroundings in ways that encourage concentration on the task at hand. Place your computer to the side and out of sight when you are interviewing. When you are training someone, put your cell phone in a drawer or leave it in another room.

The next week or so was fairly quiet for Ben. Sarah was too busy with her Silly Olympics to work with Derrick on his website, and, with soccer camp over and fall soccer still on the horizon, there were no more games or practices Ben could forget. In addition, Bobbi was out sick a few days and then afterwards decided to take a few unplanned vacation days. The thought had occurred to Ben that perhaps he had mishandled the whole change of schedule thing with her—and that that was one of the reasons she needed time away from the office—but there was nothing he could do about it now. So he went about his business.

And business was picking up. The new Face2Face campaign was showing great promise. Ben's department was discovering that many of their former customers were indeed dissatisfied with their competition and were glad to see them. It was not so much that the products they had purchased were bad as they felt no connection with their new reps. No one had called on them for years—just an occasional e-mail or text—and they felt generally neglected, almost like they were being used. Every communication was automated including their complaints and requirements.

They could not just call up a rep. They had to submit their comments and suggestions in a standard online form just so or they were "not suitable." One online form actually produced an "invalid input" message if the person filling it out used too many words or accidentally entered a non-alphanumeric character. These customers were livid. How dare these companies imply that what they had to say was invalid?

Given this experience, these former customers were amazed when Ben's reps showed up in person and asked to sit down with them. They considered it an investment in their relationship and returned the compliment, taking them out to lunch and giving them a tour of their facilities. Most of the reps loved this. They felt like honored guests, and not like irritants.

And Ben's people did just the right things—they asked questions and tried to listen to them, passing on much of what they learned to him. The only thing that worried Ben was that July's report did not show many actual sales, and the end of the quarter was coming upon him steadily. He needed to find some way to accelerate the process.

One morning, he even went back over to the accident site to see if Phil had left any more wise words to inspire him and give him direction. He did find another sign, but this one, just a sliver of wood, was so dirty and decayed that all he could make out was the phrase "quality of the day." Not much to go on. Ben leaned the new piece of wood against the others and then got back into the Equus. "Well, I guess I'm on my own," he said to himself.

Just then his phone buzzed. He had turned off the ringer and set it on vibrate just to let him know he was getting a call even if he was not going to take it. However, since he was stopped and had not really gotten very far on his way to work, he decided to take the call. He pressed the call button. Too late. The caller had already ended the call. However, he or she had left a message. "That was quick," Ben said, still talking to himself.

He then checked his messages. He had a new one from Billy's Garage and Body Shop. He had called them several times about his Lexus but had had trouble getting through. Now, at last, someone was calling him. The caller, however, presumably Billy, sounded unsure as to whether he was being recorded or not and said only that the car was ready. He then hurriedly hung up, without saying good-bye or "have a nice day" or anything. Ben laughed. "I sure hope none of my reps leave messages like that," he said, making a mental note to add another rule to his list. Perhaps showing common courtesy in a phone message was not really a way to avoid being distracted by technology, but it was still something he should remember to do. The best way he found to avoid this kind of curt confusion was to imagine the person was standing in front of him, talking to him. Therefore, he tried to speak as clearly and respectfully and as completely as he would in person.

Ben tried calling Billy back, but no one answered and no answering machine picked up. Ben was not surprised. After Billy had hauled his Lexus off, Ben had asked around and checked Billy out on the Internet—after all, he was not going to allow his Lexus to be worked on by just anyone. The scoop on Billy was that he was an extremely talented young mechanic who had worked for one of the chain auto repair shops in town. However, he had felt limited there and had decided to strike out on his own. Just like that, without a partner, without employees, without advertising, and without a readymade clientele.

And he was making it. Everyone Ben spoke with praised Billy to the skies. He had a reputation as a miracle worker, sometimes a little slow, but he fixed things other mechanics would not even try. And his body work was without peer. Most people said they stopped worrying about getting into wrecks now. Billy's work was that good—and reasonable too. No one ever complained about price gouging or whined about Billy recommending work that did not really need to be done. The guy seemed as faultless personally as was his work.

Ben instantly fell "in like" with Billy. Even though he had never met the fellow, he knew he was a great guy. Anyone who had that much initiative and was willing to risk it all on his own company with so little backing had to be marvelous. Without a moment's hesitation, Ben started up the Equus, turned it around, and drove back up Ward's Corner Road to I-275. True, he was giving up his private time to pick up his car, but Ben fully expected to be inspired by what he saw. Perhaps he would see a whole new approach, something that would get those orders coming in. In a matter of minutes, Ben was standing in front of Billy's Garage and Body Shop in Anderson. He was in awe, but not for the reason he expected.

Given Billy's reputation, he had expected a modern building, something like the BP he passed everyday on his way to work only more so—with freshly painted walls, bright lights, together with a state-of-the-art logo in front, a mini-Jumbotron, with lasers and computerized graphics, something new and dazzling, something in keeping with Billy's clean view of business, cutting edge technology, and his own irrepressible optimism. And it would be something that could be franchised and sold to other people as a package.

However, what stood before him was a garage—just like the sign said, a three-room dirty gray cinderblock building with a hydraulic lift and a lot of tools in one room, a paint booth in the other, and a small "office" in the third. It was dark. It was dingy. It was depressing. It was the opposite of everything he had expected. Instead of a well-maintained entry lined with shrubs and maybe a fence, this place sported a pot-holed path, dotted with the hulks of wrecked cars, Billy's version of landscaping, arranged in rows, badly in need of work.

Billy's Garage

Ben walked around the side to the office. There was a rusty key-drop to the side with a generic plastic sign above it announcing, in black letters of different sizes, that this was Billy's Garage and Body shop. The door was open. Ben went inside.

The room looked nothing like the thriving or even functioning business he had expected. There were no name plates or business cards, no certifications or awards, no files or computers or business machines of any kind. It was just a plain, undecorated room, more like a bunker than an office. It had a desk in it, pushed to one side, with a phone and a worn pink fluorescent paperback seemingly tossed on its surface. The book had a wrench with a flower growing out of it on its front cover. Beside the desk was a single wooden chair with a note pinned above it that read, "Assembly of Japanese bicycle require great peace of mind." Under it was another note: "Actual reality is always better than virtual reality."

Ben chuckled. "Not in this case."

Ben walked to the center of the small room and turned around, rescanning it. He did not see any clipboards with forms to fill out or calendars with work orders—just a rack of keys to the side. Ben checked the keys for dust. He started to wonder if this were really a front company for some criminals, maybe the mob. Still Ben had hope. He walked outside.

"Billy," Ben yelled. "Billy," he repeated, not knowing what else to call the owner. "Anyone?" But no one responded. Ben walked over to the door to the garage proper and peered in, cupping his hands around his eyes like makeshift binoculars. Although the room was lit, it was much darker inside than outside. Ben's eyes required several seconds to adjust. Gradually he saw the details of the room take shape—a pile of tires near a broken window, formerly stacked neatly but no more, tool chests open, their contents strewn about, a workbench toppled over in the corner—and a slumped figure in front of it.

"Hey!" Ben opened the garage door and rushed in, reaching for the man's bent shoulder, shaking him. The man instantly came to life, swatting at Ben's hands and shoving him away.

"Git your stinking hands off of me. Can't you see I'm prayin'?"

"Praying?" Ben was stunned, more from this announcement than from the man's sudden resuscitation. The man glared at him and swore.

"Yes, prayin', you dipstick. Can't a man say a simple prayer in his own garage without gettin' assaulted?"

Slowly the man stood up, using the jack beside him to help himself up. He put his hands on the small of his back and arched backward so dramatically that Ben wondered if this was part of his prayer ritual. Then the man squinted quizzically at Ben.

"Who the hell are you?"

Ben did not know what to say. The man in front of him could not be Billy. Billy, he assumed, would be older, more educated, more impressive looking somehow. This guy reminded Ben of his wild, younger brother, David—except that his blond hair was buzzed short and he had several colorful tattoos on his arms and neck: crosses, crescents, flowers, as well as six-pointed and seven-pointed stars. This man was the living embodiment of a wide-ranging ecumenicism, oddly mixed with car parts—flaming tires, pumping pistons, and angry-looking headlights drawn above a sneering grill.

"I'm Ben Rosen. I own the Lexus that was brought here about three weeks ago, supposedly to fix a headlight." Ben tried but could not keep the suspicion out of his voice.

Instantly, the man's eyes lit up. "Oh yes, 'Black Beauty.'" He seemed to temporarily go off to another more magnificent world in his mind. Then he returned. "Sorry, it won't be ready for another week."

Ben was flabbergasted. "What? But I was called. Someone said it was ready. I came all this way. It's been nearly four weeks."

The man reached back and rubbed the angry headlights on the back of his neck, contorting them slightly into a kind of wrinkled wink. "Yeah, well, sorry about that. I got this new phone the other day, and it confused me. Too many buttons. And so I called the wrong number, okay? I meant to call the guy who owns the 'Silver Surfer' in the back."

"The 'Silver Surfer?'"

"Yeah, it's a classic Pontiac GTO that was bashed into in Newtown. I just finished her last night."

"What year?"

"1964."

"An original?"

"Yep."

"A Bobcat?"

"Yep."

"Wow," Ben had temporarily forgotten all about his Lexus. "Can I see it?"

"Nope, the guy just picked her up. I'm surprised you didn't see him when you drove in." Billy went over to the pile of tires and started stacking them up, correctly, as they should have been.

Ben involuntarily glanced out the window, hoping to catch a glimpse but seeing nothing. "What color was it?"

The man spat on the floor, near the drain. He heaved the last tire on top of the stack and went over to the red tool box, ignoring Ben, and began rearranging the screw drivers. "Let's see. With a name like 'Silver Surfer' what color might it be? Blue? Red? I know, how about silver?"

But Ben was too caught up in his thoughts to notice Billy's sarcasm. "Silver. Perfect. Just the right color to show off its hood scoops." Ben then began listing its mechanical attributes, rapid fire, from memory: a 6.4 L V8, a four-barrel carburetor, dual exhaust, chromed valve covers and air cleaner, a floor-shifted three-speed manual transmission with Hurst shifter, and so forth.

The man stopped his rearranging and tried to listen to Ben, seemingly out of courtesy—or resignation. He probably just wanted Ben to leave so he could get back to work. He did not seem very impressed until Ben said that it must have been a privilege to work on such a car, just to touch it and absorb its history. "A lot of love went into those GTOs back then," Ben said. "And a lot of customizations. I think it was made to be personalized—at least that was how my Dad felt about them."

Ben smiled as he thought about all the time he and his father had spent working on the red 1967 GTO in the garage—"Ruby" they called it, naming it just like this mechanic named the cars he worked on. That was where Ben first learned about cars, working alongside his dad—handing him wrenches, listening to him explain how carburetors worked, helping him dislodge a particularly uncooperative part.

Those were good times, and he learned a lot. However, for the longest time, Ben could not figure out why the GTO always seemed to need work and why his father never seemed to make any progress. But then, after a while, while they were rebuilding the transmission for the third time, Ben discovered that it was not so much the final product his dad enjoyed—it was the process, the work, the discovery, the act of creation—and he discovered that he enjoyed it too.

At this point the man's countenance softened. He put down the handful of screwdrivers he still held in his hands, rubbed his most religious tattoos, and looked Ben in the eye. "Tell you what," he said. "Let's go have another look at Black Beauty. My name's Billy, by the way."

Billy

> *It is difficult to describe true concentration. Some practitioners describe it as feeling peaceful and completely alive, as being alert to everything around oneself yet totally focused on the task at hand. In this state of full mental and emotional engagement, other thoughts and feelings fade away and we become so focused on what we are doing that the experience cannot help but be deeply satisfying and profoundly illuminating.*

Although Ben was still not sure this was the Billy he was looking for, he followed him outside and into the painting room next door. This part of the building was immaculate inside. The other room may have looked like a landfill, but here everything was neatly arranged—the paint containers organized in rows according to the color spectrum, nozzles and hoses rolled up on hooks, and a plastic sheet, like something out of a clean room, was draped over his car, forming a hazy tent over its indistinct shape. Billy even insisted that they remove their shoes and wear special slippers inside. As a child Ben had been shown paintings of the portable tabernacle the children of Israel used in the desert during their wanderings, and this paint tent looked just like it. In an odd way, he felt as though he were on holy ground.

"Sorry about swearing at you," Billy said, suddenly serious, speaking quietly. "My dad's been working on me but that Army training is hard to overcome, I guess. Most of it, I don't want to overcome. I owe everything to the Army. It turned me into a man. I even made corporal. See."

He pointed to two stripes tattooed on his bicep. "I worked in a motor pool. They thought I had a way with machines. And I did, but I didn't know how to use it until they gave me the discipline and motivation to focus and to concentrate. I was pretty wild as a kid—always angry at something."

Ben nodded vaguely. He was still thinking of his dad and the fun they had had while working on the GTO.

Billy continued, "Some of the kids around here could use some of that Army training, it seems to me. A few of them have been coming by lately, pokin' around, and makin' noise. I didn't think much of it, until they broke in last night and made a mess of the place. Good thing the Surfer was in here, and they didn't find a way in."

Ben nodded again, this time with more clarity, now understanding why the garage next door looked like it had been bombed.

Billy walked over to the paint tent, flipped on a special high-intensity light, and went inside. His body was instantly transformed into a dark, fuzzy outline—its details both defused and highlighted by the plastic. Ben watched as Billy's vague form looked over the front end of the Lexus, bending over it, feeling the area around the head light, looking for something, testing it somehow. After a few moments, Billy stood up and waved a foggy hand to Ben, beckoning him to enter.

The light inside the tent was different from that outside, brighter, yellower somehow, more intense, and yet even in this weird light, the Lexus looked as good as new—better even. Billy had not only fixed the headlight and the damage around it, but he had touched up the rest of the car as well—filling in some tiny dents around the rear bumper and dings on the doors. The Lexus shone like the model car dealers put in their showroom.

Ben moved in front of the Lexus where Billy was. The chrome shone like silver, enhanced with gold highlights, an effect created by the strange yellow light. Its bright lines accented the Lexus' dark body, outlining a surface so pure and unblemished that Ben could see his entire upper body mirrored in it in clear detail, spiritualized, made mystical somehow as it stared back at him from the hood. Ben stood there, transfixed by beauty and a feeling of unity with his car and the world—until Billy snapped him out of it, unceremoniously flipping back one of the plastic walls.

"Well, I wanted to keep it here another day in case it needed an extra coat or something, but the paint seems to be covering the area well and it's dry and there are no signs of color mismatching or drips. So, if you really want you can take it now."

"Excellent," Ben said, now back to reality. He followed Billy out of the tent. "I was told to leave the Equus here and the rental car people would pick it up later. Is that what you understood?"

Billy either had not heard Ben or did not care. He continued moving the plastic sheet out of the way. Ben tried again.

"So, is it okay if I leave the Equus here?"

Billy seemed puzzled. "That's the plan."

"And I don't need to pay anything?"

"Nope, it's all taken care of. Just leave the keys with me."

"Do I need to fill it up with gas? It's half empty."

"Nope, that's taken care of too."

"Okay, well then here are the keys," Ben said as he tossed them to Billy. "I sure enjoyed the ride." Billy in turn tossed the keys to the Lexus back to Ben.

"Yeah well, I'm not a fan of the newer cars," Billy responded, moving over to the garage door, pulling it open. "They're mostly just a mass of components and modules. No fun to work on."

"You sound like the guy who hit me, Phil Fleischmann. He drives a really old truck." Ben noticed a shadow creep across Billy's face, just before he turned and began rearranging the hoses beside the door. "Phil's not a friend of yours, is he? I mean, that's not why you are fixing the mess he made, is it?"

Apparently Billy did not want to talk about Phil. He took down a hose and began rerolling as he stood at the open door, apparently waiting for Ben to leave.

The chaos of wrecked cars stood in marked contrast with the order of the painting booth. Ben hesitated.

"Can I ask you something?" he finally said.

"Sure," Billy said, without looking at Ben.

"So what were you praying about when I first arrived?"

Billy again acted like he had not heard Ben and continued looking out at his yard full of cars. Ben had not wanted to offend Billy—especially since he had obviously worked so hard on his car—but something about Billy intrigued him. Why was a guy so obviously successful content to work in such unimpressive circumstances? And why by himself when he could employ several people to do the mundane work and live off of their labor?

It did not make sense. There was something hidden deep within Billy that he was not letting out, some secret, and this praying of his seemed to be the key that unlocked his mystery. It was just too weird.

But Billy did not answer. He just stood there, like a statue, beside the garage door, looking down, the hose still in his hand. Ben felt embarrassed. He had overstepped his bounds. He opened the car door and started to get in. He tried closing the door but something prevented him from doing so. He looked up. There was Billy looking down on him—his eyes riveted on him, his tattoos on his arms—the religious ones—dark against his white skin, now almost bloodless as he gripped the car door tightly.

"Do you really want to know why I was praying?"

Ben suddenly was not sure. "Sure," he said, reflexively.

"Okay, here goes. First of all, it ain't because I am sick or my wife is sick or my dad is sick. I mean, they are and I pray for them all the time, just not today, just not now." Billy looked down at the hose he still had in his hands, twisting it, fiddling with it as if he were gathering his thoughts. "Fine, you probably think I'm nuts anyway, so I'll just say it. I was just thanking God for the opportunity to work on cars. That's all. That's it."

Billy then looked up at Ben, seemingly hoping for a very specific reaction. Ben did not know what to do or say.

He tried to make a joke of it. "You mean you were talking to the patron saint of auto repair?"

But Billy did not laugh. "I wish there was one. St. Christopher is about as close as anyone has come."

Ben tried humor again. He wished he had not asked. He was uncomfortable talking about religion. "You mean the saintly Brothers Pep don't qualify? I hear they can do miracles."

Billy did not even smile. Ben apologized.

"That's okay," Billy said. "I get it all the time. I'm used to it. I actually once worked for a place like Pep Boys. It was another franchise, and I just couldn't take it. They made car repair into a routine, something you put up with, something you did over and over just to make money—making up repairs and faking problems. It felt wrong but the worst part was that it was boring."

"So you are bored?"

"Me? Now? No way." Suddenly Billy's eyes flashed and his face flushed, not with embarrassment but with excitement. "You see, I know this place is not much, but here I'm on my own, away from distractions and pressures, and I get to practice my art."

"What art is that?" Ben asked.

Billy smiled. "The high art of car maintenance. You're going to think I'm crazy. Hell, you already do, but just look at this lot." Billy gestured to his field of broken down cars outside.

"To me, these cars are what a canvas is to a painter. They allow me to create and discover and learn. Working on cars is not a job to me—it's an artistic thing—even a religious thing. Every one of these cars has a special problem. They may be mass-produced on the assembly line, as though they are all the same, but they all break down as individuals. Each one is its own puzzle, its own mystery. And I just find it fascinating to discover what that mystery is and figure out how to solve it."

Ben looked at the cars—with their smashed windshields, their crumpled fenders, their rusty bumpers—

still unable to see much value in them. "Well, I'm glad you see your work that way. I'm not sure I would."

"It was probably the same with your dad. I'm not just repairing these cars. I'm customizing them, making them better, improving them, making them more individual, more unique. To me this is an act of creation, an act of God."

"Is that why you were praying?"

"Yes, I was thanking him for the vision to see my work this way. I just can't imagine how terrible it would be if I did not see it this way—as a challenge, something that took everything I had and gave me myself back again. To me it is a partnership with the universe. That is why I don't even have a radio here. I want to devote all of my experience, concentration, creativity, intelligence, and effort to the work. If I saw my job as simply replacing mufflers again and again and again, something I could do in my sleep or with just part of my mind, I'd go crazy. Giving each car my all, even for an hour or two, makes me not only good at it, it makes me joyful."

Ben noticed that Billy used the word "joyful" like a piece of candy, rolling it around in his mouth, savoring it as he said it.

"And is that why you don't answer your phone?"

"Exactly, I don't want to be distracted. These cars deserve my personal attention. Frankly I don't know how people like you do it, with your cell phones and computers and Headbook and all. Everything is so distant for you, so removed from personal contact. I would feel so torn by all their bells and whistles that I would never get anything done and I would feel so disconnected that I would not care. There would be no joy in my daily work anymore—no progress, no point, no art."

"'To improve the quality of the day, that is the highest of the arts,'" Ben blurted out, suddenly remembering a phrase from his own reading of *Walden* years ago—one that completed the quotation on the sign he had found earlier.

"'Quality of the day?' That's it," Billy said, gripping Ben's arm. "Where did that come from?"

Ben just smiled. "From a friend of mine."

"Well, will you write it down for me? I'd like to share it with someone I know. That is a really great quote."

"Yes, it is," Ben agreed and wrote the quotation down on a piece of paper he found in a stack near the desk in the corner.

"Thanks a lot."

"Thank you for your work on my Lexus." The two men then shook hands, and Ben drove off, the sharper for the experience.

Sorry, I Have to Take This

Back at the Office

> *Lack of concentration decreases our ability to do anything well. We feel torn between conflicting duties and interests. Thus we fragment our efforts and spend our strength on too many things at one time. This keeps us from functioning wholeheartedly and limits our effectiveness as well as our happiness both at work and at home.*

Ben's encounter with Billy had affected him profoundly—but not as he had expected. He had expected to find a slick, go-getting entrepreneur, a brilliant fast-talker, a whiz-kid from whom he could learn how to better finalize deals. What he had found instead was a weird kind of mechanic-poet whose unexpected eloquence had touched him deeply. Where had those words come from? Why did his eyes shine so when he talked about car repair? Ben could see that Billy had somehow found the key to a happy and productive work life—and it depressed him.

Ben tried pushing Billy out of his mind, but for several days afterwards he could not. Something about him touched a nerve deep inside Ben and he could not figure out what it was. One day Ben had to go to Anderson for something before work. He then took a "long cut" back to the office, winding along Clough Pike's wooded wilderness and heading up through Newtown, all the time thinking about Billy again and wondering what about him made him so sad.

He should be ecstatic. Billy's way of doing things was brilliant—and quite successful. When Ben was going through the stack of papers, trying to find a blank one to write on, he had noticed Billy's bank statement. The guy was loaded—and, as far as Ben could tell, he had a nearly endless stream of work to keep the money flowing in. In

107

many ways, the ramshackle garage was just a front, a disguise. Billy could afford to build his own building.

And Billy was not a Phil. He had not removed himself from society, driving around in a broken down truck, harassing people about their cell phones; he still was inside the system, working with people constructively, fixing broken-down trucks, interacting with people, in his own way. Phil may have alerted him to the danger of technology, but it was Billy who gave him hope that that danger could truly be averted. So why was Ben so sad? He did not know.

He turned left onto Wooster Pike, after crossing the Little Miami again, and headed west towards Mariemont. Ben figured on taking Muchmore, a more densely wooded road than Sleepy Hollow and his second favorite in Cincinnati, to Miami and from there onto Madeira, Kenwood, and DigitALL. He needed more time to think, to figure things out, and winding along under Muchmore's trees seemed like a fitting place to do it. However, there was some construction going on at Muchmore's intersection with Wooster, and he was forced to go to the office another way. Ben continued west, past the high school, through his old teenage neighborhood, and then onto Miami from there—right by his old house, the one his parents lived in, before the divorce.

Ben tried to avoid looking at it, but he just could not help himself. Something about the old two-story Williamsburg colonial, all brick except for some beige trim along the roof, the largest house on the block at the time, still drew him. Stuck at a stop sign, waiting for the minivan in front of him to make up its mind which way it was turning, he stared at the general features of his former home, noting how much it had changed. The general structure was the same, but the new owners had extended the kitchen area out the back and widened the garage somehow, making it suitable for three cars—none of which was a GTO. Open from the side, the now cavernous space showed clearly that his dad's pet project was long gone, as was the secret garden his mother had planted behind it. She had spent so much time perfecting it, on the sly, when she thought no one was looking. It was her only place of solace when she was upset with his father.

After the minivan finally decided to turn left, Ben turned right and gunned the Lexus up the hill. He did not like thinking about his old house or his parents. They had been such troubled people, so conflicted, so torn by disparate plans and goals and desires. He could still see them now in his mind's eye standing in the entry way, all dressed up for yet another important event—his dad exhausted, drained by the executive job he hated and was so ill-suited for, his mother looking grim, plagued by both a need for social status and a hatred for it. They always seemed so harried, distracted, conflicted by such an array of appointments, engagements, parties, and commitments, all of which they never seemed to really want to attend, that they never seemed to have time for their four children—tossing off just a quick "Be good" or " Don't do anything we would not do" as they ran out again. No wonder his brothers had gotten into so much trouble.

Ben laughed ironically. And this was during the era of antenna TVs and landlines. He could only imagine what they would have been like now. They would have been so completely overwhelmed with new concerns and additional things to do that they would have undoubtedly vibrated out of existence, wilting like the trapped Pac-Man dad would occasionally play with them at the arcade. Both of his parents, his father especially, seemed entirely unable to focus on any one thing for more than a few seconds—well, except the GTO and the garden.

Ben tried to pull into his usual parking space, the one marked "Rosen," three spaces away from the front door. However, a van was parked too close on the right and the Toyota on the other side was over the line. The Lexus would not fit. Ben stared at the too small space. That was it. His father did not fit his job. Billy was what his father could have been, *should* have been if he had had any sense—a car mechanic, a guy so satisfied by his work that it left him time and energy to attend to his family afterwards. He would not have been drained when he came home, his strength nearly spent, divvied out in little, unimportant matters to such a degree that he had none left over at the end of the day.

Ben parked instead on the other side, closer to Montgomery Road, under the DigitALL sign. The sight of it brought him back to reality. He gathered up his things and closed the door, locking it, consciously pushing his parents out of his mind. There was no point in hashing this out now. His parents were beyond his help, and he had work to do. The August reports were in and the end of the quarter was only one month away. Time was marching on, and he was no closer to his goal than he had been a month ago.

Ben got out and walked the distance into the building—striding purposefully through the lobby, up the stairs, and down the hall to his office—all the while keeping his eyes fastened on the floor, desperately trying to focus on Billy and come up with at least one thing he could use from his encounter to help him improve.

He looked up just before he came to his office. Bobbi had returned and there was yet another treat from Buskins on her desk. He hesitated, not knowing how to proceed. She would undoubtedly want to talk, tell him about her vacation and ask him about his weekend. However, he did not want to talk, not now. He therefore whipped out his cell phone, placed it to his ear, and then continued into his office.

Bobbi greeted him, cheerfully as always, and started to say something. However, Ben pointed to his phone and mouthed the word "Important call" as he moved past her desk. He then entered his office, closed the door, and put down his phone. "That was close," he mouthed again and sat down at his computer, ready to add new rules to his list. However, try as he might, nothing came. He could not get his parents' tangled lives out of his mind. They had such deep problems, even the rules he came up with so far seemed shallow and ineffectual.

Ben took a deep breath and leaned into his keyboard, unwilling to concede defeat. "Okay," he said out loud,

"Billy is somehow key to all this. What is Billy's secret?" Ben scrolled to the end of his rules document, but something about the word "rules" seemed wrong. He changed the word "Rules" in the title of the document to "Principles." Something eased inside him, clicking quietly into place.

"All right, what are Billy's principles?"

Ben started by listing Billy's characteristics. Certainly Billy was hard-working—and he was highly qualified and trained—but so were lots of people and they were not nearly as successful or as peaceful. There was something more, something other people lacked—something his parents lacked. Ben had tried to push his parents out of his mind, but as soon as he allowed himself to think of them again, the answer came: Billy had perfected the ability to focus and to concentrate. As he had said, the Army "gave me the discipline and motivation to focus and to concentrate." Ben could not seem to forget those words.

Perhaps those were Billy's principles. In fact, the more Ben thought about it, the more he saw his rules as manifestations of focusing. They even used that very word. His rules helped him keep his focus by eliminating or at least limiting all distractions from electronic devices. Ben then grouped the rules he had written under "**Principle 1: Maintain Focus**" and after it he wrote:

> **Modern technology can help increase productivity, but it can also serve as a distraction from more important tasks and provide a temptation to put off such tasks. Therefore, these devices must be used in a limited, purposeful, and disciplined way.**

He looked over what he had written. He liked the word "maintain." It implied not only that this was a management task, a way of balancing influences for optimal use, but it also suggested that this was an ongoing effort—like maintaining a car. Focusing, as he was finding out, required constant effort and frequent review.

But Billy did more than focus. He took this impulse several steps further. He had not only learned how to control his distractions, something negative; he attended to his work in a inwardly positive way—**committing** himself to car repair, consciously **choosing** to do this kind of work by setting up his own business with his own money, and, most of all, **engaging** in his work every day with every aspect himself—physically, mentally, and even, in his own way, spiritually. As Phil might say, Billy was not only "present in the present," he was also present in his work. That was his secret.

Ben thought for a moment and then typed "**Principle 2: Concentration**." He had considered the possibility that "concentration" was simply a synonym for "focus," but the more he thought about and pondered how Billy worked, the more he was convinced that this was a separate principle, the next step. He also considered calling this principle something like "Promote Concentration," because part of the effort here had to do with setting up the environment or mental attitude necessary to concentrate. However in the end, Ben decided that "maintain focus" covered that effort and he wanted to push that impulse further.

After all, Billy's was an internal effort, something that happened inside him, beyond merely controlling his outward environment. He worked within himself, within his mind and spirit, disciplining himself to be attentive, to consciously and conscientiously think only about just one thing at a time and to genuinely care just about what he was doing. He simply did not allow himself to mentally go off in some other direction. No wonder Billy expressed this principle in religious terms. In a sense it was a kind of spiritual effort that involved more than just his hands or even his mind. It was the giving of one's entire being to a task.

Ben considered what he had written and was satisfied with it. He then looked around his office and mulled over the idea of how he could concentrate on his work. Almost instantly he felt his depression return stronger and deeper than before. His office was nothing like Billy's. His walls were grasscloth, not cinderblock; his furniture was mahogany, not metal; and his tools were computers and phones, instead of wrenches and screwdrivers and paint guns.

It seemed so unreal—just like the mock-up he had made using Bobbi's interior design software--only more artificial, generic, idealized, manufactured. How could he engage his entire being in his work, as Billy did, here—in this air-conditioned hovel, soundproofed, insulated, scrupulously sanitized? Didn't such an all-involving approach require the sights and smells of leaky radiators, malfunctioning carburetors, and new paint fumes? As well as the sounds of metal being twisted, bent, and banged into place?

Ben began to feel his father's presence possessing him. He was becoming just as distracted and dissatisfied as Ross Rosen had ever been. Ben looked into his computer screen, beyond the ever-twisting, multi-colored screensaver, and saw reflected in it that same far-away look, betraying a desire to do something else besides what he was doing and be with someone else beside the person he was with. And did his hands fidget constantly like his dad's?

Ben looked at his hands. They were still, but he felt an urge in them to start doing something, anything. He clicked his mouse, dismissing the screensaver, and checked his e-mail. The reps had sent in their weekly status reports. Ben opened one. It was nothing but numbers—cold, fleshless, intangible numbers. Off in the corner he saw his mouse pointer dancing, moving rhythmically from side to side. He looked at his hand. It was doing it. It was fidgeting like his father's.

Ben got up and walked to his window. The maple was still very green, not even a hint of red in its leaves. But still Ben knew change was coming. The way the leaves whipped in the wind foretold it, twirling them around on their stems and yanking a few from their branches. Suddenly Ben knew he had to go for a walk. He needed to feel the September wind on his face and feel something real for a change. This was all too much.

On his way out, Ben passed Bobbi's desk again. He thought about using the cell phone trick again, but he had left his phone on his desk. "I'm going for a walk," he said simply, unable to think of anything better.

"Oh," was all Bobbi said. Ben thought she might ask him why and dreaded the question. He did not know how he would have responded. However, she was merciful and let him go without any further questioning.

Ben went out the back door and found a bench across the parking lot, near the trees, close to the adjacent apartment complex. He sat down. The bench was concrete and felt hard and cold, probably from the shade. He twisted around and lay on it, pulling his feet up, resting them on the end of the bench. He closed his eyes. The rays of light that made it through the leaves played upon the deep red of his eyelids, creating pulses of crimson, scarlet, and dark pink. Ben concentrated, like Billy, on the moment, focusing on the patterns that formed before his eyes, blanking out everything else.

Bobbi's Advice

> *We benefit from reminding ourselves again and again that technology exists to help us. We do not exist to help it. We should therefore find ways to allow it to do its job without letting it encroach upon what we do best. Technology should be our servant, not our master.*

"Are you all right?"

Ben opened his eyes. The light was nearly blinding, his eyes now fully accustomed to darkness. A large indistinct shadow moved into view, haloed by the sun.

"Sure," he muttered, feeling embarrassed, twisting himself back into a sitting position. "I was just ... uh ... oh, it's you."

"Yes, it's me," Bobbi said taking a seat beside him, flipping her fragrant red hair, her hand again dangerously close to his. "Are you okay?"

Ben folded his arms around himself, pretending to be cold. "Yeah, I just needed to think something over. That's all. And this seemed like a good place to do it."

"Oh so you think better when you are lying down on hard cement, outside, with your eyes closed and your feet up? I'll let the physical facilities people know. They can rearrange your office for you in a new style. What do you call it? Early Stone age?" Bobbi nudged him, teasing him again, like she used to.

Ben took the bump but did not return it. Ben looked down at his hands. "Sorry, I guess this is kinda odd behavior, isn't it?"

"Not for someone who dances in conference rooms, it isn't." She started humming the chimney sweep song.

Ben could feel himself blush. "Yeah, well I'm sorry about that. I didn't mean ..."

"No, I'm sorry," Bobbi interrupted. "I'm the one who acted improperly, remember?"

Ben nodded. "Yes, I do." He could feel that hug even now and, considering how down he was feeling now, it felt good. Despite himself, he smiled a little.

His smile, however slight, seemed to give Bobbi courage. "So, when are you going to fire me?"

Ben sat up straight in surprise. "Fire you? Why? When? What for?"

"Why, for hugging you, of course," she said matter-of-factly. "I was out of line. I overstepped my bounds. It was just that, well, I was so concerned that the meeting would be a flop and that things would go badly for you in front of the reps that when you told me everything worked out ... well, you know little over-enthusiastic me. I just couldn't help myself. I just had to hug you. I was so relieved. Sorry."

Ben relaxed his back. He felt some of the tension in it ease. "No, I'm not going to fire you. You're too good. I ... this place ... would fall apart without you."

Bobbi seemed tremendously relieved at this news, too relieved. Ben felt another hug coming and to prevent it turned his attention again to his hands. They sat in silence for several minutes. Finally Bobbi spoke.

"Then why are you so distant?"

Ben felt her turn towards him and lean a little closer. He looked at the grass in front of him already showing signs of recovery from the summer heat. "I'm not distant." Some of the tension in his back returned.

"Yes, you are. We used to talk all the time, but now you hole up in your office in the mornings and always seem to have something else on your mind when I see you—something you have to do, like talking on the phone or typing or something. You seem very far away these days, Ben."

Ben thought about the cheap ploy he had employed that morning. "Sorry, I ...." He hesitated, not convinced he should complete his sentence. He still did not trust Bobbi entirely, despite her explanation and apology. There was still something about her that seemed to crave a close connection—maybe the kind of connection Sarah and Derrick had.

However, Ben did not know what else to do. He had to open up to someone, and she was here, claiming her only interest in him was professional. He took a deep breath and looking directly into her eyes, told her about Mr. Shaw's bet and how he was afraid of losing his job.

"That's ridiculous. No one runs a business based on bets. Not even 'El Shaw' would do that."

"Who?"

"'El Shaw.' It's what Mendez calls Mr. Shaw sometimes. She gets so frustrated with him that sometimes she even says she wishes 'El Shaw' would die, but she doesn't really mean it."

"Well, I hope not. No one should say that."

"I know, but you can see why she gets so upset. This would just be idiotic. I mean, you are doing a great job. We've made our numbers two out of three quarters, and there is still a chance this quarter will come through."

"Maybe."

"There is no maybe about it. We've just got to work harder and ... well, I am sure you will come up with something."

"That's just it," Ben went on. "I don't think I have it in me. I don't seem to be managing things well. Maybe I'm just not meant to be a VP or even a manager. Maybe getting fired would be good for me and allow me to go back to selling."

"What?" Bobbi whooped even louder, her voice echoing off the building's surface and around several cars. "You? Not a good manager? No way. You're the best sales manager there ever was. You have a way with people, of inspiring them, of concentrating on them, of engaging them like no one else I know."

"How would you know?" Ben said, embarrassed by the volume of her words and entirely unconvinced by her tone.

"I've heard people talk," she continued. "You are a legend around here. No one else can sell the way you can. You notice things about customers and their needs that no one else does and then you figure out how the products can help them. It's like every person is a customized challenge for you, and you don't do it just to make a buck. You honestly want to help them and that comes through."

"Is that really what people say?"

"Yes, and you know what else they say?"

"Sure," he responded dryly, steadying himself for more over-the-top praise. Billy was right. Reality is always preferable to virtual reality, even when it came to compliments. In the end, they felt like dust in his mouth.

"They say this manager's job has ruined you. They say you have gotten away from what you are good at and have changed. You're no longer the same Ben Rosen you were. There is no swagger in your step any more, no confidence, no buoyant personality. They say you are on your way out."

Ben was stunned. He could feel anger coursing through his veins like a drug, intoxicating him, taking him over, pouring out from within. "Oh, so I was right. I am not right for this job. Thanks a lot, Bobbi. Thanks for nothing. I think I will just stay on this bench now, until winter comes and I freeze. What do I pay you to do anyway?" He turned away, feeling more like his father than ever before.

Bobbi leaned over, grabbed his arm, and swung him around. Ben twisted his free arm, attempting to break her grip, but Bobbi hung on. Hers was no caress or affectionate squeeze. Her hand felt more like an eagle's talon, her nails digging into his bicep, hurting him. He had no idea she was so strong.

"Listen," she said, her face now inches from his, her eyes wide and intense. "You pay me to assist you. That is why I am your administrative *assistant* and not your secretary. In my professional opinion, you are the greatest sales manager there ever was, or at least you could be. Your problem is that you have lost your focus. You think your job is to concentrate on reports and forms and figures and other administrative things. But you're wrong. That's my job. Your job is to train and teach and inspire—people things, not number things."

Bobbi grabbed Ben's other arm, just as tightly, and shook him some in the process. "Ben you need to use me." She blushed, realizing how her words might sound, but immediately shook it off. "You know what I mean. I can help you, if you let me. You may think you are the corporate executive type, but I have a message for you—you're not. You're a people person. That's your gift. You're not a number cruncher or a policy pusher or a techno nerd, like me. And the thing is, the more you try, the more you let yourself and everyone around you down. Ben, you've got to refocus and concentrate on what you're good at. You've got to give people your full attention and leave the details to me."

Bobbi then let go, her energy spent. She looked again at the grass under her feet and then kicked at it with her toe. "Sorry, Ben. It just pains me to see you doubting yourself like this. You've got so much to offer. And, well, if you keep going on like this, I hope you do fire me. I just can't take this any longer, seeing you like this."

And with that, Bobbi touched his arm one more time, stroking it this time, caringly, tenderly, but more sisterly than like a lover. And then she left, leaving Ben to his thoughts.

Ben did not remain on the bench long. Bobbi's words had hit him like a slap in the face, smacking him harder than the cold wind. She was right. He was off course. He was not like his father. At one time he really enjoyed his job and was devoted to it—especially at the beginning. He had thought it was the new car, the nice suit, the spacious office, and, of course, the money, which was finally coming in after their years of struggling as students. But today he realized that this was not so. It was the people—the customers he interacted with daily, the reps he teased and playfully competed against, the manager he revered and attempted to copy, even the programmers and engineers he met with in order to make their products more in line with what customers wanted.

In a way he *had been* like Billy—not as isolated, of course, or as tattooed or eccentric—but just as focused and just as devoted to his work. People were what he concentrated on. They were his "cars." He was not repairing them, obviously, but he was constantly thinking about them, pondering their likes and dislikes, getting to know them, and attempting to serve them. In this way he was continually working on them—tinkering on his relationship with them, souping it up, fine-tuning it so that they all worked perfectly together and purchased a lot of product from him.

But fundamentally it was not the money that motivated him. It was the thrill of discovering a new need, a fresh possibility, and in creatively filling it in a way that made everyone happy. In this way, he was like his father, in his garage, transcending a problem and making something better. That was why he liked working with his dad—as well as talking with him and others about cars. It was not the cars themselves. It was these shared feelings. In the end, cars were just machines.

Ben soon left the parking lot and trotted back to his office. He had an idea and he could not wait to start working on it.

"Administrative Assistant Blake," he addressed Bobbi formally, standing at attention in front of her desk. "I hereby formally request your assistance."

Bobbi laughed, and saluted him. "At ease, Boss Rosen. What do you need assistance with?"

"I have changed my mind about conducting rep evaluations over the phone and have decided to conduct the remaining ones in person." Ben paused for effect. Bobbi's smile broadened. "Therefore will you contact the reps in Pittsburgh, Buffalo, and Cleveland, and set up a reasonable schedule for me to see them next week. I will be driving and would like to spend a day with each of them. I can leave this Sunday, if that is best."

"Yes, sir. Excellent idea, sir. Wish I had thought of it, sir. Is that all, sir?"

"Yes, I leave all the details to you. But we have to move quickly. We have only four weeks left in the quarter."

"Thank *you*, sir," she said, emphasizing the "you" and saluting him again. "I will get right on it. I won't let you down. I'll find you the coldest caves, the rawest meat, and of course, the meanest women around."

"Don't push it, Bobbi," Ben said winking at her.

"I won't, sir. Mental note: no pushing. Yes, sir. Got it."

"Good," he said, winking, and then he saluted her back, snapping his heels and doing his best imitation of the "vibrating arm" salute he has seen the British soldier do on *The Bridge over the River Kwai*. He then went back to his desk, flipped open his laptop and brought up his Rules (now Principles) document. Under "Principle 2: Concentration" he wrote:

> **First of all, figure out what your work is fundamentally and learn to devote all of your attention to it. This is especially true if your work involves people. Remember to concentrate on them and not on the tools you use to reach and to teach them. Do not be distracted from this, your primary purpose.**

Ben then spent the rest of the day calling each of his reps, complimenting them on something they had done recently and apologizing for his unsupportive behavior and for undermining the point of Face2Face. After all, he had wanted his reps to show their former customers how much DigitALL still cared about them and their business by visiting them personally—by meeting them physically, without the intermediary of electronics, and by spending time with them. And yet, he had done the exact opposite. He had only contacted the reps via those same devices and therefore showed how little he cared about the campaign and about them.

Most of the reps were shocked by his call, confused by this sudden show of personal attention. Some were even suspicious, asking him what they had done wrong and if a layoff was coming soon. However, Ben won them all over in the end and they even opened up about some of the problems they were having but had been afraid to tell him before. Ben was amazed at how the words just seemed to come to him and how experiences he had had as a rep seemed to inspire and instruct them. He should have done this a long time ago. Something had held him back, something he could no longer remember.

At the end of each call, each rep thanked him profusely and said how much the call meant to them—especially the reps he had planned to visit next week. All three were very excited and looked forward to introducing him to their customers. They were sure it would be an extremely positive experience.

Sarah, however, did not agree.

Sarah's Response

> *The myth of multi-tasking is most apparent in our relationships, both at work and at home. Facebook may not mind if you answer an e-mail while you examine your home page. The report you are writing may not care if you monitor the temperature outside while you type away. But people, real people, do mind if you answer a phone or text others while you are talking to them. The discrepancy between what you appear to be saying ("I am interested in you") and what you are actually doing (showing interest in something or someone else) comes across as hypocritical.*

"Why would they care if their boss visited them or not?" Sarah said, slamming the groceries on the kitchen counter, ripping the bags. Organic eggplants and squashes along with canned goods and cereal boxes spilled out onto the granite surface. "I don't care if the principal visits my dodgeball class or not. It doesn't make me a better PE teacher. In fact it would make me worse."

"Yeah but this is sales. These people are all there alone in some city, doing their best to hawk our wares as best they can. They need my support, and it's just one week."

Sarah turned and looked him in the eye, her eyes blazing, the groceries entirely forgotten.

"Yeah well, *I* need your support. Don't you realize what goes on around here in a week's time? Amy and Aaron both have soccer games and soccer practices and then there are school projects and music lessons. Did I tell you Amy wants to be in a school play? Well, she does, and it's after school. Therefore, she is going to need to be picked up because the buses don't run then. I can't do this alone, Ben. Your children need a father who is present sometimes."

Ben winced. "No, I didn't know about that." Ben started to help Sarah pick up the groceries, but she slapped his hands away, seemingly preferring to do it herself.

"I added it to my Facebook status over a week ago. Didn't you get a message?"

Ben backed away some. "I may have. I don't know. Sarah, I get so many e-mails these days that I just can't keep up."

Sarah slammed her hand on the counter. "But from your wife? Surely, those get your attention—more so than e-mails from Barbie."

"Bobbi," Ben corrected her out of reflex and instantly regretted it.

"I don't care what her name is. Or what she does. I need help here. I just can't do this all by myself. And on top of everything the virus is back. I can't even get online anymore. I have to do everything at the school." Sarah staggered a bit and moved her hands to her temples, closing her eyes. Ben could feel a migraine coming on.

Ben was teetering. Perhaps this was too much. Perhaps he should change his plans. Two days is not much notice. Perhaps he didn't need to go this coming week. Perhaps he could go later or limit his tour to two cities instead of three.

In an instant, Ben had all but decided to tell Bobbi to bag the entire trip when Sarah added that she and Derrick still had to finish their video. "Our regular training sessions on Tuesday and Thursday afternoons are just not enough. We're going to have to meet on Wednesdays as well."

At this point whatever sympathy Ben felt for Sarah and her situation suddenly disappeared—and he yelled at her. He actually yelled. For the first time in their marriage that he could remember, Ben exploded, railing not only on Derrick but on Sarah, her mother, father, and anyone else connected to her that he could think of.

Ben then stormed out of the kitchen, leaving Sarah to pick up not only the scattered groceries but the hateful words he had spewed everywhere like water from a broken faucet. Not knowing where to go, he went into the family room where Amy and Aaron were playing a video game on the big flatscreen in the dark, oblivious to their parents. Ben plopped down on the couch beside them, noisily, as though he were staking his claim.

"Dad" Aaron whined. "You made me run off the road."

"You were losing anyway," Amy taunted. "Don't use Dad as an excuse."

"I was catching up. You always slow down around the curves cuz you're chicken."

"I am not. I'm just not as reckless as you are." Amy seemed pleased with her big word.

"Are too," Aaron retorted.

"Am not."

"Are too."

"Am not."

"Kids!" Ben yelled, still smarting from his conversation with Sarah but beginning even now to regret his words. "Be quiet. Can't a man have any peace in it own house?"

"It's all Aaron's fault," Amy explained. "He started it."

"Did not."

The childish back and forth nearly resumed again before Ben interrupted. "I get it. I get it. Just start the stupid game over and this time race against two other cars. Pretend you are a team."

Ben watched, his guilt growing, as they dutifully added two more cars to the field and restarted the game. It did not take Ben long to see that Aaron was right—Amy did slow down in the curves—but Aaron frequently accelerated when he should have slowed and banged into the virtual guard rails frequently, losing points, and thus hurting the team. Aaron was out of control.

As Ben sat there, he saw himself mirrored in Aaron's red Ferrari. He too was out of control—getting off track and crashing against things. He shouldn't have yelled at Sarah like that. She was right. She needed more help. His kids needed more help. Just last night, when he had come home late, he had found her lying exhausted on the bed while Amy and Aaron were attempting to "study" while watching *Jurassic Park* and texting friends. He did his best to explain rationally why this kind of multi-tasking did not work, but ended up confiscating their phones. Dealing with kids like this all day, no wonder Sarah was worn out.

And Derrick? How was her relationship with him any different than his with Bobbi? They were just colleagues after all. Perhaps there was some romantic tension there, but Sarah was capable of sorting it out. She was a big girl and a devoted wife. He should not be so suspicious.

Midway through the second race, Ben decided to break the ice. He took out his phone and texted Sarah. "im sorry" and after a few seconds he added: "im a pita."

Sarah had told Ben about this abbreviation a few weeks ago. As a teacher of pre-teens Sarah prided herself on her knowledge of slang and more recently of text lingo. She often sat her students down and let them teach her the words they were using these days. It was one of the ways she tried to relate to them and make them feel validated and welcome in her classes. And she enjoyed it. To her it was just another one of her invented games—like baskervoll, only with words.

Ben waited for a response. None came. He tried again: "ioii"—meaning, "intelligent outside, idiot inside." He reversed the usual abbreviation for "Intel inside, idiot outside." He was not sure he was using it correctly, but he still hoped Sarah would find it funny. It certainly encapsulated how he felt.

Still no response.

"no lol? i really am sorry. im just feeling a lot of pressure. too much to do and deadline is closing in. I going crazy."

Finally she responded: "crz?"
Ben was confused: "?"
Sarah: "it means crazy"
Ben: "oh"
Sarah: "no oic for oh i see"

Sarah's Response

Ben: "oic"
Sarah: "ihbd2d2"
Ben: "what?"
Sarah: "i had a bad day 2 day 2"
Ben: "you made that one up"
Sarah: "ynk"
Ben knew that one. It meant "you'll never know."
Ben: "lol"
Sarah: "kidz r pitas"
Ben: "r kids?"
Sarah: "nw skol kids"
Sarah: "r kids r gr8"
Ben: "yes, they r"

Ben looked over at Amy and Aaron, both bent over their controllers, shifting to the right and then to the left in unison as they desperately tried to pass the other cars, their faces the image of focused concentration, oblivious to everything else around them.

Ben went back to texting Sarah, continuing with their word game. He was beginning to understand why Amy and Aaron, like most kids, were addicted to texting—there was something seductive about it, something intimate, something all-involving. It was like a video game only real. He felt like he was sending secret messages to Sarah on the sly, encrypted notes only she could understand. It was like Sarah and he were the only people in the world.

Ben felt himself melt, his rage dissolving gradually with each intimate text he received. He was such a fool. He had so much. Sarah was such a wonderful wife and his was such a wonderful life. Ben looked up at Aaron and Amy, now high-fiving each other as they celebrated their victory, ready to race again. It was such a small thing, a simple suggestion that had changed their view of each other. But they still required continual care and instruction. It was just too much to ask Sarah to do it all herself. He had to do more.

Ben chuckled to himself. He could not wait for the next time they started doing their homework while attempting to

127

watch TV and text friends. He was ready for them now. Armed as he was by his experience with Phil and Billy and charged up by Bobbi's challenge, he could not wait to explain to them the benefits of focusing and truly concentrating on one thing at a time—and he was going to do it face-to-face, personally, without distractions or while thinking of other things. Funny how adults can see the obvious dangers of multi-tasking for kids, but rarely for themselves. Perhaps kids are right—adults are hypocrites, at least in this way.

But no more. Ben smiled. He was going to do it right. He was going to be their example. Ben felt a cocoon of goodness enfold him, spun by this secret conversation with Sarah. Something about texting seemed to shut out the rest of the world, its problems and concerns, and put everything in its proper perspective. He loved Sarah and his children and that was all that really mattered. He felt so connected to her right then.

Ben went back to text on his phone and tried to explain to Sarah his plans, not just for the kids but for himself—what had happened at work, his experience with Billy, his thoughts about his father, his depression, even his thoughts on the bench and Bobbi's advice—but it was just too much.

As intense and private as texting had been, it only seemed to work for concentrated messages, short bursts of thought and feeling, ideas that could be reduced to single lines or standard abbreviations. Texting was just not designed to handle complex feelings or longer, more complicated situations. In a way, he felt like he was talking through a keyhole. He could look through it and see some things more clearly, but relating all of the thoughts this sight conjured up was impossible—not through such a limited medium. His thumbs simply did not work fast enough.

After a few frustrated attempts, Ben finally stood up, excused himself (his kids did not even notice) and started to look for Sarah. He was going to talk to her personally, husband to wife, intimately, privately, in a concentrated way, just as he planned to do with his reps only more so.

After a few seconds of looking, he found her in the dining room, just thirty feet away. She was sitting at the table, surrounded by papers and a calendar, cell phone in hand.

Sarah looked composed now, even happy as she punched out her next message to him—her thumbs fairly flying over the small keyboard, never seeming to pause or correct mistakes. All anger had left her face. She was even smiling, laughing almost. Sarah was certainly older, but at that moment Ben saw again the same beautifully intense college student he had caught sight of in the library so many years ago and fell in love with instantly. He saw her stop, seemingly done with her message. He moved back, away from the doorway, and waited patiently for her text to come. He thought that he would surprise her by jumping out and answering it personally.

But nothing came. After a while, Ben peeked around the corner and saw Sarah still hunched over her phone, working her thumbs all over it. Again, she stopped, again Ben waited, and again nothing appeared on his phone. This continued for several more minutes. Finally Ben figured out what was going on. He slipped around to the other entrance to the dining room and came up behind her, quietly so he could see her phone without her seeing him. One glance was enough to confirm his suspicions.

Sorry, I Have to Take This

Pittsburgh

There is no higher compliment to someone than giving that person your undivided attention. And the compliment comes back to you. Attending to a person in a single-minded way not only builds the self-esteem of that other person, it also helps you better express yourself and hear what that other person has to say.

Ben was relieved to hear that Steve could meet with him a day early. After his fight with Sarah, he needed to work. He needed to concentrate on something else besides her. He also needed to do something about the looming deadline instead of worry about it.

Ben walked downstairs into the hotel lobby and checked it out. It was perfect. Its leather chairs were arranged drawing-room style, in small groups, around low-lit tables and tall plants. In the center was a fireplace, a hearth, surrounded by harvest-themed knickknacks, making the entire room seem warm and cozy and inviting—just the right kind of place for a supportive training session.

Ben went into the hotel restaurant and picked out four particularly sumptuous-looking pastries and arranged them carefully on a plate. He also grabbed a handful of napkins and a pot of coffee as well as two mugs. He placed them all on a tray and then made his way back into the lobby to a corner that had looked particularly promising. There he positioned his goodies in the center of a table and pulled two of the most inviting chairs around it, on either side—not opposed to each other in confrontation but placed side-by-side, each inclined slightly towards the other, the way colleagues, equals might sit as they chatted in a relaxed manner about things in general.

Ben sat down in one of the chairs and poured himself a cup of coffee. Everything was ready. He sipped his coffee and prepared himself to push everything else out of his mind and concentrate solely on Steve, his Pittsburgh rep. For sixty minutes, he told himself, this lobby would be all that existed in the universe. There was no "outside." It would be just the two of them—colleagues teaming up to make this sales area as productive as possible. Ben slid his laptop and a legal pad off to the side of his chair, out of sight. Now all he had to do was wait for Steve to arrive. But waiting proved difficult to do.

Across the lobby, two families—one dressed apparently for church, the other looking more like they were on their way for a drive—walked past. Their kids slapped at the large schefflera in the hallway and made loud tap dance noises on the tiled floor. One, a girl, started singing just to hear her voice echo and another, a boy, jumped up and down, tugging on his father's sleeve, desperately pleading for some favor. Ben could not help thinking about Sarah and the kids, and the adventures they used to go on when they were smaller. Despite himself, he wondered how they were doing and how they were taking the news that he had left on his trip a day early.

How would Sarah break it to them? Would she put her own slant on his actions? Would she cast him as the villain for not being available for their usual Sunday activities—kicking the soccer ball around in the yard or driving off somewhere on an impromptu adventure?

Ben smiled as he thought of how they had all gone to the Museum of Natural History & Science a few weeks ago. For some reason they had pretended they were Neanderthals reacting negatively to all the press the dinosaurs got in the first exhibits—shaking their heads in disbelief as they read how they dominated the earth long ago and running around the model of allosauruses and such, mocking their all-too-apparent slowness.

Ben had wondered if they were actually making fun of the museum itself, hinting that they were too grown up for such childish things. However, when they entered the Ice Age exhibit, through the fake ice tunnel and into a room of amazing detail, both of the kids went crazy, hopping up and down like apes, grunting their excitement. This was their epoch, a primitive time of giant musk oxen, bison, and saber-toothed tigers. Aaron pretended to throw imaginary spears at the wooly mammoth stuck in the muck and Amy too got in the act, and at one point ran up to the giant sloth and excitedly cried out, "Momma." Everyone cracked up, even the normally staid museum workers.

Ben took out his phone, thinking he might give them a call, just to reassure them that he was still thinking of them. However, the sight of his phone reminded him of why he came to Pittsburgh a day early. "How could she?" he asked himself again, for the 90th time. "How could she, after all they had been through, be so hurtful?"

Ben put his phone away. He had thought about Sarah and Derrick all the way from Cincinnati—speeding along first I-71 and then I-70, basically daring the highway patrol to pull him over—and no matter how hard he tried he could not understand it. It seemed like such a deliberate act of betrayal, such a conscious undermining of their relationship and the trust they had. Sure, she had not slept with Derrick or even kissed him, as far as Ben knew, but it still was a blatant two-timing, an electronic form of infidelity that made him sick to his stomach every time he thought about it. Even the pastries across from him—glistening with cream cheese, cherries, blueberries, and kiwi—did not look good to him now.

Ben stood up and began walking around the lobby, muttering to himself, trying to regain control of his thoughts. Perhaps Derrick had initiated the conversation and perhaps he did urgently need her opinion about some photos he had taken of her exercising. Ben understood deadlines and the need to get more than one thing done at a time, but this was different. This was personal. There was no call for him to say those things about her or her body or for her to entertain them as she did. It was just not right, not right at all.

People can't, or shouldn't, have intimate conversations like that with two different people at the same time, not like this, not with Derrick. Ben opened and closed his fists reflexively—opening them again almost from sheer will.

Maybe Sarah was right. Maybe this was just the way Derrick talked, the way he talked to everyone. Maybe he didn't mean anything by it and maybe neither did Sarah. But still it felt to him like emotional hypocrisy, like she was only pretending with him and really cared more for Derrick. It cast into doubt their entire relationship, all the years together. Maybe she had been pretending then, too. Maybe she had just been waiting for someone like Derrick to come along.

Ben realized he was not thinking rationally. Perhaps it was the job stress or lack of sleep or something, but he could not shake it. For the first time in their married life, Ben was not sure who he was married to. He felt like his entire world was falling apart.

Yes, Ben told himself, work was what he needed right now—hard, demanding, all-consuming work, the kind Billy had, the kind that Billy enjoyed. Ben glanced out into the parking lot, looking for Steve but seeing only cars. More than anything, Ben wanted right then to be a car mechanic. He wanted to spend all day under a car, hidden away from his problems, banging on a too tight exhaust pipe with a hammer or yanking on some stubborn bolts with a wrench. He longed for the sweet smell of antifreeze or the feel of warm oil as it oozed over his hands. He needed something physical to do, something multisensory, something to fix his mind and his heart and his hands on. He needed to concentrate. The problem was he just could not.

"Hi Ben." Steve strode into the lobby, several minutes early. "Thanks for driving out all this way to see me. I didn't know you cared."

The words shook Ben out of his thoughts and brought him back to reality. He stood up and greeted Steve warmly, with a firm, two-handed handshake. Despite the self-absorption that still dominated Ben's thoughts and feelings, he could tell that Steve was nervous. After all, it was fairly obvious. Despite his initial bravado, Steve's hand trembled slightly when he shook it, and he stumbled over his next few words, mumbling something about everyone knowing that Ben really did care—despite his inability to show it well in his e-mails and messages.

The more Steve tried to explain his comment, the worse it got. Finally, he just stopped talking altogether and smiled sheepishly.

Ben looked Steve over, attempting to read his face, wondering what he had to be nervous about. He tried to smile reassuringly, doing his best to seem humble and in earnest—earnestly humble, as he called it. "Actually, I am sure all that is so. I need to show that I care better."

Steve's smile disappeared. "No, you are the best. I was just kidding. Everyone knows you are the best boss in the country—I mean the world. You are the best boss in the world. Yes, that's it—the world."

Steve looked away, seemingly as a break, and looked down the hotel hallway. "Nice place you got here. So, where shall we go? Do you have a conference room? I have all the usual reports with me, and then some." He patted his briefcase.

"Let's just stay here," Ben said as calmly as he could. He was still not sure what was going on with Steve.'

"Here?"

"Yes." Ben motioned for Steve to take a seat beside him.

"Okay, as they say, you are the boss, the best boss."

"Thank *you* for coming so early and on a Sunday too. I know you probably have more interesting things to do on a Sunday morning."

"Not me," Steve fairly spat. "I live for work, for DigitALL, for you."

"Coffee? Danish?"

"No thanks," Steve said, taking his seat. He fumbled with his briefcase, awkwardly attempting to unlock it and not managing it. His hands were shaking. Ben reached over and stopped him.

"That won't be necessary, Steve. That's not why I came."

Steve closed his briefcase with a loud click. He took a deep breath. "I know. You came here to lay me off, didn't you? I heard rumors, but I never. ..."

"No, no," Ben exclaimed, waving his hands as though erasing the thought from the air. "Nothing like that. No. Heavens, no. Not you. How could you think that? No, I'm just here to see how things are going, and to help in any way I can. That's all. Is that all right?"

Steve nodded yes, but still seemed unsure. "So you came all this way just to talk?"

"Yes—and to see if I can help some."

Now it was Steve's turn to stare at Ben. "Wow, the department must be in real trouble."

Ben laughed. "Well, we could be doing better, but that's not really why I'm here. I just want to see how you are doing. So," he paused, "how are you doing?"

It was simple question, not particularly brilliant or probing or original, but Ben was amazed how effective it was. Steve was hesitant at first, even suspicious, but seemingly thinking that he had nothing to lose, that his dignity had already been compromised, opened up—talking rapidly initially but then slowing to a steady, heartfelt, sincere pace.

And Ben did his best to encourage him. Remembering a few insights into body language that he had read about on the Internet, Ben followed up on the atmosphere he had attempted to create by making sure that his knees pointed towards Steve and that he leaned in to him to hear him better as he spoke. Ben also nodded encouragingly occasionally and cocked his head to the side, inquisitively, while keeping his eyes fixed on Steve and keeping quiet—

only occasionally asking short, open-ended questions and expressing his understanding of what Steve was saying.

This approach seemed awkward at first, especially when he glanced down at his notes to make sure he had not forgotten anything. Ben felt stiff and phony, like he was putting on an act or playing a character. However, as Steve talked what he told Ben was so interesting that he soon forgot all the things he was supposed to do and just did them, naturally, without thinking. In many ways, Ben forgot all about himself and any concern he had about how he looked and lost himself in what Steve had to say.

And this was rightly so. As Ben discovered, Steve was truly an amazing person. He was quite impressed by all the innovative things Steve was doing to get to know and connect with his customers—things that went far beyond what Ben had told him to do—as well as his knowledge of DigitALL's products, knowledge that in many ways eclipsed Ben's own.

After a few minutes, Ben stopped Steve and explained that he just had to write his ideas down, that they were so good he wanted to share them with the department. He pulled out his legal pad from beside his chair and began jotting down notes. As he did this, Steve went silent and for a second Ben wondered if he had broken some important body language rule, never break eye contact or something. After all, he did not remember his Internet advisor recommending note-taking.

However, as it turned out, Steve was just waiting for him to catch up. Ben looked up from his paper and stared at Steve. He was looking at him with an expression of supreme pleasure and gratification. Steve seemed complimented that Ben was taking what he said so seriously and thought highly enough of it to want to tell others about it. After noting what Steve had expressed, Ben wrote down a note to himself:

Show your interest in the people you work with by taking time to talk with them individually in a comfortable setting, one that promotes a sense of security and mutual respect. Make eye contact and truly listen to them, and demonstrate that you take them seriously by taking notes on what they say and by acting on their comments.

Ben added this last line because as soon as he started writing he realized that he was making a commitment. His notes were a kind of contract that he was signing to do something about their ideas. Just looking at Steve's ideas made it clear that he would be very disappointed if Ben did not actually send some of them out to the other reps—or mention them in a department meeting. Yes, that was it. Ben added "have Steve and others present ideas in next department meeting" to his notes.

When Ben stopped writing, Steve started talking again, describing his efforts with even more vigor and detail and stopped occasionally for Ben to catch up. At one point, Ben added to his personal notes: **"And they often have really good ideas."** Ben was truly impressed. He had thought that he was going to have to train his reps on the most basic fundamentals of customer relations, going over all the aspects in an effort to fill in whatever they were missing.

Now he realized how unnecessary it was—and how harmful that would have been to his reps' morale. Sure, he added a few tips but he mostly listened and discovered that Steve knew a lot and even came up with ideas Ben had not thought of. Giving him the Sales 101 course would have squashed his confidence and probably destroyed his enthusiasm for DigitALL. This way Ben got more ideas and he did not have to work as hard—since he could concentrate on a few things. Mostly what he needed to do most was to encourage the reps and keep the lines of communication and appreciation open.

The hour passed quickly. Ben was completely absorbed and excited with what was going on. He had forgotten completely about Sarah and their problems as well as everything else. He was concentrating fully on the task and person at hand. Then his phone buzzed.

Without thinking, Ben put down his pen and reached for it. Out of the corner of his eye, he saw Steve's face. It had changed dramatically in just an instant. Gone was the enthusiasm and joy that had been there previously. He looked to the side, and down. He seemed smaller somehow, sunken, darker.

And there was something in his expression that reminded him of something, someone. Yes, it was how he felt when he discovered that Sarah had been texting Derrick while she had been texting him. There was that same sense of betrayal in his face, that same loss of confidence in a previously trusted person, that same feeling of disappointment that Steve was not getting Ben's full attention, that Ben somehow had his mind and heart elsewhere, even partially.

It was just a momentary impression, one that zipped by in a nanosecond and could very well have been incorrect. Nevertheless, Ben decided to act upon it. That feeling of betrayal was so strong with Sarah that he did not want Steve or anyone to feel that way, even to a reduced degree, with him. He pulled his hand back and let the thing buzz.

"So, what were you saying?" he asked Steve, his pen poised again above the paper and his eyes again fastened on his face.

"Oh," Steve exclaimed. "I thought you were going to take that."

"It's nothing. Probably just Mr. Shaw asking my advice about some corporate policy again," Ben joked. "Happens all the time. He can wait."

Steve laughed and leaned in with even more earnestness. His knees were now pointed very much in Ben's direction and his eyes were also fastened on Ben's—unconsciously sending out all the signals Ben had initially performed consciously. Steve was very interested and engaged—and what is more he seemed to feel trusted and appreciated. His smile and vigor had returned threefold.

After his meeting with Steve and setting up a time for them to visit customers the next day, Ben went back to his hotel room. Immediately he opened up his laptop and began adding his notes to his principles list. In addition to what he had already written, he added another rule—again dealing with concentration:

> **Never take a phone call or even look at your phone while in conference with another person. This will seem like an emotional betrayal and will show a lack of interest in that person and in his or her ideas. In addition, as you are listening to that person, take occasional notes on what he or she is saying and consider how that person or activity helps your larger goals. Not only will that person feel more valued and appreciated, but you will be better able to use those ideas to further your goals. In the end, everyone gains.**

Ben then closed his laptop and considered what he might do for the rest of the day. Perhaps he would take in a museum or even a ball game. It had been a good day already.

More Interviews

> *In successful human interactions, nothing can replace face-to-face communication. While technology can enhance, supplement, and encourage such communication, it should not supplant it.*

The next day, Monday, Steve picked up Ben and drove him to see a few former customers Steve had already contacted. Ben was amazed at how friendly Steve was and how enthusiastic he was to take him around. Ben was also thrilled to make two very important discoveries.

For one, he learned how little he actually had to do. Simply accompanying Steve worked wonders. All of the customers Steve took him to see seemed to be teetering on the edge of committing. They just needed something special to push them over the edge. Ben was that something special. As they saw it, the fact that a VP, even a junior VP, would come all this way just to see them was a huge compliment and showed a deep commitment to them as customers.

Basically all Ben had to do was compliment Steve, affirm DigitAll's confidence in him, and Steve did all the rest. After that, commitments were easy to obtain. Two people signed up for service that day.

Secondly, and most importantly, Ben discovered that the same behaviors that impressed Steve impressed these customers. They too were thrilled to receive personal, undivided attention—and responded well to his note-taking and open-ended questions. As an experiment, Ben kept his phone turned on and arranged for Bobbi to call him during his last customer visit in Pittsburgh. As he had done with Steve, Ben made as if to answer it and then, with more show than he had demonstrated with Steve, waved it off, showing as well as telling their customer that she mattered more to them than some phone call.

And just like Steve had been, the customer was extremely pleased. It was almost as though Ben's sincerity was being put to the test and by leaving the phone unanswered he had passed. As a side note to his principles list Ben later wrote:

> **Cell phones can be great helps to sales personnel—especially ignoring them. During sales calls, cell phones are inclined to be bothersome gadgets which distract our attention from more profitable things.**

Ben thought that both Phil and Billy would have approved, and perhaps even Thoreau too—although perhaps not.

Ben left Steve that afternoon and drove up to Buffalo. His time there was like déjà vu all over again. Again, Ben met a very nervous Sean O'Reilly and reassured him that he was just there to see how things were going and to help. Again, Ben listened carefully and took notes and found that Sean too had tried some interesting approaches—ones that Steve had not. And again, he promised to showcase his ideas in the next department meeting and was greeted by great appreciation and gratitude. Ben's experience with former customers was also repeated. Again, he complimented Sean in front of each customer, had Bobbi call him in the middle of each meeting, and again each customer beamed when he ignored the call.

Things were going well. Already his trip was a success and he was starting to feel that they could actually become the most productive region in the company. Several former customers had inked deals then and there while a few others were on the verge. They just had to check with their chief systems engineer or financial officer or some such person. The department's goal was within reach—Ben could tell. It was going to be tight but things were on the move.

Ben still had not talked to Sarah (although he had texted her that he had arrived safely). But perhaps that was best, he thought. All these thoughts about her and Derrick were dragging him down, distracting him from his work. What he needed to do now was to concentrate on these reps and keep himself focused on the quarterly goal. That was what was missing. That was why he was not yet like Billy. He just had to have more faith to let things go. Once he got to that point, Ben was sure everything would work out somehow.

On Thursday then, Ben was in Cleveland, waiting at a TGI Fridays for Jill, his rep there, to appear. Jill, for some reason, did not want to meet at Ben's hotel and instead proposed this spot. Ben laughed at the idea, suggesting that she was already hoping that it was Friday and that their time together was already over. It was probably not a good joke. He meant that she was probably eager to have him leave, but he thought it came off as if he was eager to leave.

Jill certainly did not think it was funny—at least she did not laugh. Of all of his reps, she was the most serious—and most productive. But she was also the hardest to read. She never called him or requested his help. She was almost completely self-contained, drumming up orders week after week, as if by magic. Ben honestly wondered if he had anything he could teach her. She was that good.

Jill entered the restaurant three minutes before their scheduled meeting and, after only a moment's scanning, found him in a corner booth next to a window. Ben waved but it did not seem necessary. She bee-lined towards him, head down, as if she were on a train track. He readied himself for a collision.

"Morning, Mr. Rosen. I hope I did not keep you waiting." She stuck out her hand and shook his with a firm but still feminine handshake. Ben motioned for her to sit across from him, which she did.

Jill was impeccably dressed, as usual—with her neatly tailored blue suit, black closed-toe shoes, and expensive-looking scarf and pin. She looked like a Wall Street lawyer or investment banker. Even without knowing anything about her, Ben would have pegged her for a fast-tracker, someone who was going to rise up the ranks at DigitALL or some other company. Everything about her seemed efficient, calculated, and economical. There was no wasted movement with Jill. Still, she seemed too cold, too robotic for Ben. As far as Ben could see this was all that was holding Jill back from conquering not only Cleveland but the world. Sales reps, even the hyper-competent, needed some warmth about them. Ben decided that the best way he could help her was to help her relax more, to loosen up, to relate to customers in a more informal way.

"Well, Jill," he began, with a wry smile. "This is not the start I had expected. After all, you kept me waiting—for *fifteen* seconds. This is just not like you. Are you slacking off?"

Jill did not laugh or even smile. She looked stunned. "I'm sorry, sir. It will not happen again." She took out her phone, checking it, thumbing something into it, probably taking notes.

Ben waved her off. "I'm kidding, Jill. No one is as punctual as you. You were actually early. You're the best rep I have."

Jill seemed somewhat relieved but continued to fiddle with her phone. This time Ben was not pleased. Perhaps she was taking notes to use against him.

"You can put that thing away, Jill. We are all friends here."

"Yes, sir." She carefully placed her phone back in its specially designed pocket on her laptop case.

Ben folded his fingers together and leaned over the table. "Don't customers joke with you, Jill?"

"No, sir. Mostly they just talk about business—servers and orders and such."

"Don't you find that a little too impersonal?"

"No. Not at all. I know their business operations and they know what I can offer them as a DigitALL representative. I think it's very personal."

Ben sighed. He could tell he was getting nowhere. "Okay, then. I'm sorry. I don't mean to criticize. You really are the best. I was just trying to make you even 'bester.'"

"I don't think that's a word, sir."

"You are right. I was out of line. I'm sorry. I won't do it again," Ben said, but he was not entirely telling the truth. There had to be some way of loosening her up. Customers just could not feel comfortable with her. If she would just open up more, then perhaps she would be the best rep in the entire company.

"So, what customers do you have for me to see today? Oh and by the way, I'm not here to lay you off."

"Excuse me?"

"I'm not here to lay you off. The other reps thought that was the reason why I visited them and I had to reassure them that I was not before we could get down to work. And so I'm also reassuring you as well."

Wow, Ben thought, if that is how a "loose" rep talks, then Jill is certainly right to stick to her approach. Still, if she made him nervous and caused him to fumble his words, then it is highly likely that she had the same effect on customers. There had to be some way to help her.

Jill looked at Ben for a second, frozen, as if she were trying to figure out how to respond to his wild words. Apparently she decided the best course of action was to ignore them. "Just three, sir. Two are fairly routine and then I have one with Ms. Namath."

"Ms. Namath?" Ben asked lengthening the Ms. into a kind of cicada-like buzz. "Does she play football?" Ben laughed at his own joke, but Jill did not react. He was not doing well at all.

"Ms. Namath is the owner and CEO of Zephyr Corp. They produce a wide variety of health-related products—ranging from exercise equipment to vitamins to skin care products, all of which they make available to customers in customized 'packages,' which include tele-consultation, online support, and personal training. They were a large customer of ours several years back, but something

145

happened, and they went with one of our major competitors."

Ben smiled. In all of his discussions with Jill, she would never mention the names of any of their competitors or any advantage their products had explicitly. She would talk about them indirectly and was quite knowledgeable about them, but she never used their names. Ben could not tell if this was an odd quirk of hers or just good sense.

Jill again ignored him and moved on. "As I was saying, Zephyr is now reconsidering their earlier decision and seems inclined to switch to us. Ms. Namath heard that you would be in town and wanted to meet with you personally to discuss some details."

"Excellent," Ben said, pounding his hand on the table in a desperate attempt to add some human feeling to their discussion. "Let's get going then. I'm sure you have done such a good job with her that all I have to do is sit there and endorse what you have told her. Soon the deal will be done and I will be out of your hair."

Ben was trying to explain his earlier joke but he was again not getting anywhere. He was beginning to look forward to Friday. This was going to be a long day.

"Honestly, I'm here just to show you that I care about what you are doing and to learn from you. Again I'm not evaluating you or checking up on you. There are no lay-offs on the horizon. You are clearly our best sales person."

"Thank you, sir," Jill replied. "Ms. Namath is a very shrewd woman. She oversees all the major purchases her company makes and something is keeping her from signing with us. I've met with her several times and explained our products to her, but I am still not sure what it is. I am hoping you can help."

Ben again slapped the table enthusiastically. "Well, let's find out, shall we?" He jumped up and with an exaggerated flourish of arms, bowed. "My car is at your disposal, m'lady." Out of the corner of his upside-down eye, he saw Jill smile, just a little.

At last, thought Ben, I'm making some progress.

Zephyr Corp

> *Companies can do much to encourage their employees to devote all their attention to their work at the office or factory by allowing them to similarly devote all their attention to personal matters when they are at home. Such a division though no longer necessary technologically is still vital psychologically. If work is something that now exists in cyberspace, employees must be freed from that work when they are at home, even if that means having separate cell phones and e-mail accounts.*

The first two interviews were indeed as Jill had described them, routine. As with those in Pittsburgh and Buffalo, the customers seemed very pleased to see him and responded positively to his ignored phone call ploy. Jill had also prepared them well and they were eager to sign. Her command of DigitALL's products was impressive as was the work she put in to showing how they could help these companies in their individual circumstances. Ben had never seen such technologically-rich selling before.

However, Jill was still stiff around them, almost uncomfortable. When Ben attempted to talk to her about this, when they are alone in his car, she did not seem to listen, going on and on instead about Ms. Namath and her concerns about her. Jill seemed consumed by her and her company.

As soon as Ben laid eyes on Ms. Namath, he knew why. She too wore a well-tailored suit, just like Jill although grey not blue, and sported a colorful scarf and a gold pin on her lapel. Her shoes were also close-toed and matched the red-leather handbag she had set off in the corner. In many ways, she looked like an older, wealthier version of Jill—perhaps a vision of what Jill would become later.

"Ms. Namath, Mr. Rosen; Mr. Rosen, Ms. Namath."

"Pleased to meet you, Mr. Rosen," Ms. Namath said, with properly pursed lips, shaking Ben's hand, Jill-style.

"As am I to meet you." Ben even bowed a little when he said this. Jill glared at him out of Ms. Namath's sight. But he could not help it. Ms. Namath seemed so formal, so stuffy, in an almost regal contemporary/Victorian way—like her office. Everything about it seemed the ultimate of overdone business elegance—dark walls, rich cherry furniture, modern twisty lamps, and art—real art, not reproductions—in expensive frames on her walls and in her bookshelves.

Ms. Namath walked past them and took her seat behind her large cherry desk. "Please be seated," she said, indicating the two leather-upholstered chairs directly in front of her desk.

Ben and Jill did so, and as he sat down, Ben noticed the credenza behind her desk. There were no business awards or trophies on it. Instead it was full of photos, also exquisitely framed, surrounded by mementos—vases, flowers, small antiques—all apparently associated with the people in the photos, most of which looked too happy to be employees. They must be family—or friends—since there were no photos of Ms. Namath with a Mr. Namath, at least as far as Ben could tell.

"Mr. Rosen?" Ben's attention was jerked back to Ms. Namath. "Jillian informed me that you were coming today. Perhaps we can do some business together to our mutual benefit."

"I hope so," responded Ben, instinctively. Ms. Namath looked away momentarily, and Ben mouthed, "Jillian?" Jill, however, was not amused.

"Ms. Namath?" she said when Ms. Namath turned her way again. "I have a short presentation I have prepared for you that I would like you to see. It concerns several

DigitALL products I think would fit well into the Zephyr business model, perhaps even improve it."

"Very well, but first we must have some tea. Mr. Rosen, would you care for some tea?"

Ben declined, but Jill accepted her offer. Ms. Namath buzzed her secretary, and told him to bring in tea for two. While they waited, Ms. Namath "entertained" them with stories of her latest trip to Europe with her sisters, a few photos of which were on the credenza behind her. Ben did his best to appear interested, but it all seemed too pretentious and affected to him. This was Cleveland, after all, and they were here to do business. And what did Westminster Abbey have to do with WANs anyway? Or the Louvre with LANs?

Still, Jill seemed captivated by Ms. Namath's effete travel log. She even asked several probing questions and expressed a desire to see what she called the "Lake District" where Wordsworth had lived and worked. Ben stared at Jill. He never knew she had any interest in anything outside of a circuit board.

Once the tea arrived, Ms. Namath offered milk and sugar to Jill, prepared her own, and then, once she was comfortable, asked Jill what she had for her today. Jill set her tea cup aside and produced a folder of very colorful charts, a glossy presentation she seemed to have expressly created for Ms. Namath. She then proceeded to detail the advantages of employing DigitALL to service a midsized company's intranet rather than their competitors'—companies which, Jill-style, she referred to as Companies A, B, and C.

The presentation was impeccably organized, thorough, and tailored to Zephyr Corp. Ben could tell that Jill had spent countless hours preparing it—doing research, talking to DigitALL's developers as well as to Zephyr Corp's own people, and arranging everything just right. Jill reinforced the subliminal point of her presentation by stressing the responsiveness of DigitALL's service to Zephyr's needs and emphasizing several times how Zephyr and DigitALL would be working closely together, especially to make sure that the transition to DigitALL servers would cause only a minor disruption to Zephyr's day-to-day operations.

Ben was extremely impressed. However, as far as he could tell, Ms. Namath was not. She gazed at Jill skeptically throughout and, though attentive, tapped her glasses rhythmically against her pursed lips. She seemed pleased but unconvinced. And Ben thought he knew why.

"Jill is not making up these figures out of the air, by the way, Ms. Namath. They come from our competitors' own evaluations, evaluations that are readily available on their own websites and confirmed by independent test groups."

Ms. Namath, turned to Ben, her glasses momentarily still, looked him over, and then turned back at Jill. "Is that so, Jillian?"

"Yes, ma'am. However, I was saving that for later." She then handed Ms. Namath a sheet of beige paper with several URLs neatly printed on it with the real names of companies A, B, and C in parentheses.

Ms. Namath replaced her glasses on her face, glanced at the URLs, and then turned her attention back to Jill. "Thank you, Jillian. I very much appreciate your thoroughness as well as your discretion. No need to be beastly competitive about all this, is there? Please continue."

"Yes, ma'am." Jill replied and then reviewed the array of services she was suggesting as well as several pricing options.

Ben was not sure what had just happened. However, he could see that Ms. Namath was in fact interested and engaged with what Jill was telling her. It was clear that they were on the same wavelength and that he was not—so he resolved to stay out of Jill's way as much as possible. He simply did his best to make sure his body language showed him to be interested and sincere. He was not dumb, after all.

Several minutes later, however, Ben's phone buzzed, surprising not only Ms. Namath and Jill but Ben also. He felt for it awkwardly in his pants' pocket, unsure as to what to do. Bobbi was not supposed to call him for another five minutes, and he was not expecting a call from anyone else. Ben fumbled for his phone for a few seconds but then decided to ignore this call, just as if he was planning to do when Bobbi called. But Ms. Namath would have nothing to do with this.

"Mr. Rosen?" Ms. Namath said. "Aren't you going to take that?"

"No, ma'am," Ben returned, reciting his usual speech about no call being as important as a conversation with a valued customer. Ben then turned away from Ms. Namath and winked at Jill surreptitiously. He knew what was coming next. Unfortunately it did not come.

"Well, you should have thought of that before you left your phone on," Ms. Namath said, looking directly at Ben, her glasses pointed right at him. "Please check your phone, Mr. Rosen. I'll wait."

"It's okay, ma'am. You're more important." Ben sat back, pleased with himself, waiting for the usual response. But it did not come.

"But it could be an emergency. Someone could be ill or hurt or worse. Here at Zephyr Corp. we don't as a rule allow non-emergency personal calls during work hours. So, if someone calls, we figure it must be an emergency."

Ben again protested. Ms. Namath again insisted, and so, feeling pretty sheepish about his subterfuge, Ben reached into his pocket, pulled out his phone, and looked at the caller ID.

"Oh, it's nothing. Just my wife."

Ben looked up to see both Jill and Ms. Namath glaring at him—one in fear, the other in horror. Their eyes focus on him like loaded shotgun barrels.

"What? I'm sure it is nothing important. Really. Probably just some little thing about the house or the kids. It's okay. It's nothing. She can wait. She's used to it."

"Mr. Rosen," Ms. Namath began, putting her glasses aside and leaning meaningfully over her desk. "I'm not sure how your company is run, but here at Zephyr Corp we respect familial as well as business relationships. We are a health company, after all—a *holistic* health company, a company founded on the principle that human beings are multifaceted creatures. We therefore feel that our employees as well as our customers are not simply cogs in some machine."

"Look at these people." Ms. Namath gestured to the photos behind her. "They are wives and husbands, mothers and fathers, daughters and sons—a whole array of relationships and responsibilities, all of which need to be respected if we are to be healthy, fully functioning human beings. In fact here as Zephyr we don't even call them employees. They are all partners."

"I see, well, commendable but I ..."

Ms. Namath continued, pointing to Jill, who was by this time discreetly collecting her materials, preparing herself to leave. "Look at your wonderful colleague Jillian here. She is supremely competent and qualified and totally devoted to her work. We Zephyr partners are just like her—during work hours. We are passionate about what we do. However, we understand—no, we embrace—the fact that our partners have much to do outside of work that, when attended to properly, actually makes them more productive partners as well as better people."

Ms. Namath leaned back in her chair, smiling slightly.

"Did you know, Mr. Rosen, that Jillian is a trained ballerina and that she teaches modern dance to eight-year olds on Wednesday nights?"

Ben looked over at Jill. "No, I, uh ... well, that is ..."

"I thought not. You probably also do not know that she is a devoted aunt and sister. In fact, she vacations with her sisters every year at a new national park. The Everglades it was last, I believe. And they have done so for four, no, five years. And not only does that keep her healthy in mind and body, but it also makes her an ideal sales representative for Zephyr Corp. So everything balances out in the end. Balance, Mr. Rosen, that is what Zephyr is all about.

"We therefore respect our employees' right to have a life outside of work and actually require that they leave work behind when they leave for the day or go on vacation—no reports, no e-mails, not even phone calls. Granted, emergencies happen, but since we do not allow personal correspondence or phone calls during work hours, we figure that it is only fair to similarly forbid business correspondence or phone calls after it.

"In other words, Mr. Rosen, to us our wives *are* important—very much so—and so are our children and our sisters. We do not ignore them nor do we expect our partners to ignore them. And, as a result, our partners are happier, healthier, and more productive than employees in other companies. This is the Zephyr model, Mr. Rosen, one that we are based on and proud of. We are more than just a collection of products and services, sir. We are an approach, a way of living, which just so happens to help us create excellent products and services. Who we are outside of work influences greatly who we are inside of work and to a large degree determines the quality of that work."

Ben did not know what to say. He had never been spoken to by a customer this way before. But Ms. Namath was not finished. She pointed her glasses directly at Ben and continued.

"You are free to think of me as an old dried up, divorced, bitter crone if you wish, but I have had to learn these things the hard way, and if you keep up this Neanderthal approach of yours you may very well lose that wife of yours to someone who values her more highly and will take her call for help."

And with that, Ms. Namath turned to Jill, apologized to her, in mild tones, for her outburst and then dismissed them. The interview—or audience, as it seemed more like—was over.

Sorry, I Have to Take This

I-71

> *Technology can provide the illusion of progress while actually impeding it. When we receive countless e-mails, status notes, and texts, we may therefore feel busy and engaged with many people and on many fronts. However, much of this "busy-ness" accomplishes little business. Too often, it is the mere spinning of one's wheels: great effort expended without much movement. Success is guaranteed by concentrating our efforts on our goals and on the people important to those goals.*

Ben was in shock after his meeting with Ms. Namath. He mumbled an apology to Jill for ruining her presentation and for not measuring up as a boss, and then went back to his hotel, canceling the other business calls Jill had set up. Ben had managed to compliment Jill, something he had planned to do even before he arrived—part of his "encourage the troops" effort—but the words came out hollow, without much feeling or conviction, more like an explanation of his apology than a pep talk.

Ben had checked out mentally. Not only was the quarterly goal in question, but the idea that his devotion to his job—all of his efforts to make Sarah comfortable and provide her with all the luxuries he thought she deserved—had actually wrecked their marriage—driving Sarah away from him into the sweaty arms of that derelict Derrick—consumed him. He went right up to his room, closed the curtains and lay on the bed in the dark until sleep finally, mercifully, came to him.

The next morning, Ben felt better, more energized. He got up, shaved, showered, and put on his suit as usual. But the interview still hung over him like a cloud. He checked his phone.

He had two messages—one from Bobbi, the call he was supposed to have gotten during the interview but missed, and the one from Sarah, which he still had not heard. He selected the call from Sarah and listened as she haltingly described her need to talk to him when he returned about "a decision she had made about them."

Ben immediately shoved his phone into his pocket and began gathering up his scattered clothes and stuffing them into a bag. He felt sure he knew what the decision was and that it concerned Derrick and her going off with him. But maybe there was still time. Maybe he could still salvage something of his life after all. But he had to act quickly—and dramatically. He texted Jill about needing to leave because of an "emergency at home," got into the Lexus, revved it up, and started off for Cincinnati—still without eating.

The day was foggy, much like Ben's mind, and only got worse as he drove. He drove robotically, following the misty signs back to I-71 and then south, paying little attention to anything around him. Ben had no idea what he was going to say to Sarah. No witty saying or snappy excuse came to mind. He could think of no way to fix this. The more he thought about it, the more the problem grew in his mind. It had gone on too long. It seemed like too much of a part of him. He had no idea how he could be both himself and a good husband at the same time. The two things seemed unalterably opposed—like oil and water, never to mix. "It's all my fault. It's all my fault," he kept repeating, sometimes as a statement, sometimes as a question. Either way, he felt condemned.

However, about a hundred miles south of Cleveland, near Gahanna, the fog lifted, the sun came out, and Ben started to see things more clearly.

"No," he suddenly said out loud to the rear of the Toyota Tundra in front of him. "It's not my fault. Ms. Namath is wrong. She does not know me. She does not know Sarah. She does not know our situation." The Tundra did not respond.

"And she was totally out of line to speak to me that way. It was unprofessional. Who does she think she is? The Queen of Cleveland? The Empress of Ohio? And what a stupid way to run a business."

Ben went over in his mind all the times he saved deals because he happened upon a last minute e-mail sent after work hours or took a customer's call on the way home from work or agreed to go to dinner with clients to discuss their reservations. This wall she had erected between work life and home life may work for her factory "partners" or her service providers, people with clearly defined hours, but for sales people? No, such a thing was impossible.

Again, the Tundra did not respond. It just continued on, silently blocking his view of what was ahead of him. It even seemed to slow down some for no reason Ben could see. Seeing an opening to his right, he zipped into the slow lane and managed to sneak by the Tundra when a Ford Focus ahead of him sped up and opened up a space between them. As he passed, Ben glanced over at the Tundra. A German shepherd in the backseat bared his teeth at him and barked at him aggressively.

"No, we sales people have to be on our toes at all times," Ben said, this time to the Tundra's front bumper. "And sometimes our families have to suffer a bit and sacrifice—and just persevere. It's part of the deal. It's part of the cost of living well. Lots of people do it and manage just fine."

Ben bared his teeth at the German shepherd and growled at it. "Yes, it's a dog-eat-dog world out there where everything is in a state of constant motion. You gotta keep moving. You gotta stay aggressive—on top of your game—or you get run over and eaten." Ben chuckled at his mixed metaphors. "Everything is always changing, all of the time, especially with technology—but the nature of the beast remains the same."

The Focus slowed again, and Ben tried the same move on it. However, just as he was about to pull ahead of it, the pickup ahead of him, red like Phil's only newer, suddenly slowed, allowing the Focus as well as the Tundra to surge ahead, leaving Ben stuck in the slow lane, trapped behind a line of cars that seemed to stretch back a mile. As the Tundra passed him, the German shepherd looked down on him, panting, its tongue out, seemingly laughing.

Ben decelerated, following the pickup's lead, and waited for an opening. One came about three cars after the Tundra. Ben instantly zipped into the space, hitting the gas and then the brake in quick succession, just enough to match the speed the cars in the fast lane without hitting the one ahead of him.

But it did no good. The progress of the line of cars almost immediately stopped. The fast lane slowed to the speed of the slow lane, and everyone bunched up, running almost bumper to bumper. He was trapped. There was nothing he could do. He could not even see what was causing the hold up—probably a semi trying to pass another semi—but who knew? All he could do was drive on, keeping his eyes riveted on the truck just inches ahead and wait for something to happen.

Ben hated waiting. He hated waiting for servers to notice him, for cashiers to ring up his purchases, for people to answer his calls, for the kids to get ready in the morning, for Sarah to get ready for bed. There was just so much to do, especially if he was going reach his goals. That is why Ms. Namath's approach will never work. There was just too much pressure. Work could not be simply left alone while he played with the kids or chatted with Sarah. That's the way people get stuck and businesses fail.

Sure, it was okay to devote an hour every day to thinking over things without interruptions. But that was different. It was still a business activity. He was still working even if he was not answering his phone or responding to e-mails. Leaving all those things unattended without doing something productive was giving the

I-71

competition an opening, and that was all it took for them to win.

Ben glanced behind him. In his mirror, he could see a classic Corvette, the kind with roll-up headlights, nearly parked on his rear bumper. It flashed its lights, signaling him to get out of the way. Ben stood his ground. He was not going anywhere. The Corvette would just have to wait as well. The Corvette, however, was having none of it. Suddenly accelerating, it somehow found an opening in the slow lane and wedged in between him and the cars ahead.

Ben was furious. He considered speeding up and perhaps even bumping the 'Vette as it shifted into his lane. But he just could not do it. Safety issues aside, it was just too beautiful a car to mar in any way. However, now the Corvette was ahead of him. Its sleek bumper seemed to sneer at him, mocking him with its taillights, humiliating him much more that the German shepherd ever could. Ben began to rethink his decision not to bump the Corvette and actually starting pushing down on his accelerator, testing it. However, instead he pulled over into the slow lane, taking the space the Corvette had evacuated, just to be away from it. He then adjusted his speed to match the plodding semi ahead of him and resigned himself to a long stay there.

"See, Ms. Namath," he said, this time to the semi's rear doors. "See what happens when you aren't on top of your game all of the time? When you don't push ahead every moment of every day? You get left behind, or worse." He stared at the silent steel doors. "Maybe Sarah would not be having an affair with Derrick if I worked for a company like Zephyr. But I don't think so. Here in the real world you can't separate home and family. They get tangled up. That's just the way it is. One second's lapse and that's it. You're not in business any more. I did this for her."

Ben then drove on, following the semi, lost in his road-rage misery—hating it and the Corvette and the Tundra and the Ford with all of his heart but unable to do anything about it. The cars seemed to pack around him even more tightly. However, since nothing was happening, he decided

159

to call Bobbi, to see if the department was at least making some progress. She had to be in the office by now. She answered briskly.

"Hey, Boss. Where are you?"

"Hey Bobbi. I'm a little south of Columbus, on my way home."

"Already?"

"Yeah, something came up and I had to leave. I will tell you about it later. Right now I need to know how this week's sales went. Have the reports come in?"

"Most of them. Do you want me to give them to you?"

"Please."

"Over the phone or by e-mail?"

"Over the phone. I can't wait for e-mail."

"Okay," she said, taking a breath. "Here goes. But I'm warning you, it's not as good as we had hoped."

"Go ahead. Nothing could be as bad as this traffic," Ben joked.

But Ben was wrong. True, the news was not completely bad—they were still awaiting reports from Milwaukee and Chicago as well as Cleveland—and the numbers for Pittsburgh and Buffalo were up—showing that Ben's trip had helped, some—but on the whole what he heard was not encouraging, especially since the end of the quarter was just two weeks away.

Ben thanked Bobbi and hung up. "Well, I guess I could turn around and go to Chicago and take in a few more areas around there." Ben was talking again to the loading doors of the semi in front of him. "That might help some."

However, even if he helped bring in a few more accounts, losing others like the Zephyr deal because of his interference would not only cancel them out, it might sink him as a manager. Even though he had apologized to Jill, he could tell that she was glad he was not going with her on any more calls. He had probably destroyed any trust she had in him—at least for now.

No, what he needed was a miracle—and a big one too.

I-7 1

Ben laughed at himself. A miracle? Had it really come down to that? Was he really that desperate? Immediately Phil's first quotation popped into his mind: "The mass of men lead lives of quiet desperation."

Ben shook his head and stared at the big aluminum doors of the semi in front of him. So, after all that he done to wrest control of his life back from cell phones and Facebook and e-mail and the other "pretty toys"—as Phil had called them, quoting Thoreau—he was back where he started—on the road, rushing to work, confused, not knowing what he was going to do next, and well on his way to being fired. Was all this progress a distortion, like the car in his side mirror?

No, Ben glanced at the BMW behind him. It was closer, not farther away, than it appeared. There had to be a way. He was just not seeing it. Again Ben thought of Phil and about his warning about cell phones and such keeping him from seeing things as they really are. He must still be distracted in some way. All this work could not have been for nothing. He had made so much progress. This was not a mirage. There had to be a solution—a logical, reasonable, practical solution—right in front of him. Ben focused on the truck's doors and concentrated on his problem, forgetting all else, leaving the driving to his muscle memory.

Ben reviewed in his mind all of his possibilities, including somehow restoring an account himself, somewhere in Cincinnati. Sure, it would mean infringing on someone else's area, but maybe that could be forgiven under the circumstances. He could call it a grandfather deal, something left behind from his previous work—an exception, an anomaly. It would be all right. However, Ben, despite all of his ethical wrangling, could not come up with a name. All the old customers he remembered had either already renewed their interest in DigitALL or were irrecoverably attached to one of their competitors. He had, after all, tried this once before, before the current push.

Ben continued to stare at the shiny aluminum doors of the semi in front of him. His way was blocked and locked.

There seemed to be no way around them. Until that very moment, Ben had never noticed how large the latches on semi trailers were or how massive the padlocks attached to them seemed.

Despite his best efforts, Ben's mind wandered. He wondered what could be so valuable inside to merit such precautions. The doors looked thicker than those on other trucks, and they were insulated. A small hatch was open on the back, showing what looked like two inches of extra insulating material. Other than that, the doors were blank. There was no writing on them other than the weight of the trailer and some warnings about closing the doors properly before moving.

Below the doors was a rusty license plate, battered by some chance collision. It reminded Ben of Phil's plate, a piece of metal just as rusty and worn. Phil again. For some reason Ben could not get the old broken-down hippie out of his mind. Perhaps their paths there linked somehow, cosmically, joined like comets orbiting a star, out of sight for a time but ever returning.

Perhaps he was going to end up like Phil. After Sarah divorced him and DigitALL let him go, he too might end up driving around the east side of Cincinnati, in an old truck, waiting for distracted people to hit him and then collect their insurance. It would not be such a bad gig. Maybe he could juice it up some and buy a neck brace or crutches—maybe even a wheelchair. He still had one from when Sarah broke her leg a few years ago while showing her kids how to climb ropes. The insurance settlements alone would keep him sitting pretty for years.

Ben glanced again at the Mercedes still following closely behind him and wondered briefly what might happen if he touched his brakes. At the very least he could get a new car out of it—maybe even an extension on his goal from Mr. Shaw if he got hurt. No, that would not work. Mr. Shaw thought that even dead people should keep on selling. As he said once, sales people don't die—they are just reassigned.

I-71

That was the weirdest thing about Phil. He had it all set—it was even clearly Ben's fault. Why then did he not take the money and run? He could have feigned injury, and his truck was so beat up, the slightest bump would have totaled it. So, why did he claim the whole thing was his fault—and pay for everything? And where did he get the money to pay for all this? He even got an Equus, no less.

As Ben was thinking about Phil, the semi signaled and exited I-71. As it slowed on the off ramp and Ben zipped by, Ben glanced at it. The bright metallic trailer caught the sun for a moment and flashed radiant in the still early light. Ben looked away, but before he did, he saw clearly on its side: "Fleischmann's Yeast. Active Dry, RapidRise, and Pizza Crust." The words now burned into his retinas.

Ben punched the accelerator. It was a sign.

Sorry, I Have to Take This

The Fleischmann Estate

> *Businesspeople sometimes forget that they, as well as their clients, are people and as such must be treated as people—not as machines or computers or websites or message-generators. Any approach that promotes a single-sided view of oneself or others is doomed to failure. People have many sides to themselves, and recognizing this promotes holistic development and enjoyment.*

Ben had often thought about visiting the Fleischmann estate. Frequently, after a tough day at work, he would drive by several Indian Hill mansions—Ambleside, Three Knolls, the Hoffman Farm, Four Winds—to remind himself why he was working so hard and what he hoped to accomplish. It was his pre-Billy way of refocusing himself, of concentrating on his work.

He would not actually approach these mansions or knock on their doors. He would just drive by, slowing his Lexus to a crawl, and look them over, drinking in their grandeur and absorbing their grace. Sometimes he would park beside them and, with his eyes closed, imagine himself sipping cognac before a carved stone hearth, leafing through a rare first-edition in his cavernous library, or just ambling with Sarah through their manicured grounds.

And the cars they'd have! Ben would nearly drool over the prospect of owning his own Rolls Royce, Aston Martin or Bugatti—maybe even all three. His garage would be huge, nearly the size of a warehouse, with a sealed floor, showroom lighting, and its own lift. A mechanic would come around once a month just to check on things and to make sure that each car was running perfectly, purring like a well-fed cat.

These were wonderful thoughts and they helped motivate Ben to work harder, concentrate more, and push himself, but they were fictions. Try as he might, he never could believe that he could ever actually own any of them. Mr. Shaw could pull himself up by his bootstraps, leaving IBM with a small package, risking his life savings on a start-up, and believing so fervently in that start-up that he poured himself into it, completely, until it blossomed into the success that DigitALL was today. But not Ben.

Ben simply did not think he had it in him to do that well. He was not smart enough or smooth enough or devoted enough to really make it big, and that was apparent whenever he considered the Fleischmann place.

It was different from all the other mansions he knew. It was so far beyond even his most optimistic imaginative reach that it exposed all of his faults and failings. It depressed him. He would look at photos of Winding Creek Farm on the Internet—this three-story, Normandy-style, stone manor house with thirty-five rooms, an indoor swimming pool, elaborate gardens and extensive grounds, including stables, horse pastures, a greenhouse and acres of woods—and try to picture himself somewhere inside them, but he just could not. It was simply too much. The sheer size of the place crushed whatever fantasies he had. Only true financial giants dared to walk its halls—people with names like Carnegie, Vanderbilt, and Rockefeller—certainly not a Rosen.

Ben once came across a photo of Julius Fleischmann in front of his great house, preparing for one of his famous foxhunts. Beside him were other, lesser millionaires—the owners of the homes Ben had visited—all sitting proudly on their thoroughbred steeds, each resplendent in his scarlet coat and white breeches, smiling, joking, drinking wine, surrounded by hundreds of hounds, all baying away, eager for the chase to begin.

These were true aristocrats—nothing like that royal-wannabe Ms. Namath. They all looked so happy and so relaxed. However, when Ben zoomed in, he seemed to catch a glimpse of another very different picture. At 150% he seemed to see it in their eyes, the way they glanced sideways at each other, sizing each other up, even during this seemingly social event—squinting, methodically searching for some weakness or advantage that they could exploit. At 200%, Ben could see the same thing in their fingers, in the way they held their riding crops and reins—seemingly calm, but actually tense, almost twitching, ready, eager, to send this mass of men and beasts racing furiously after their quarry, driving it on, unremittingly, to its death.

These men were consummate competitors, winners so dominant that they no longer had to compete to survive. And yet they did, for sport, for fun, for amusement, as something to keep their finely tuned skills sharp and their senses ever-alert. They hunted not because they had to or even wanted to but because that was who they were—predators, apex predators, men so focused that for them only the hunt existed, the process of devoting all of their considerable talents to one thing, a goal, and reaching it at all costs. They were like Billy on steroids. And Julius Fleischmann was the most dominant of them all.

And so Ben avoided the Julius' estate. After all, what would Ben say to the descendants of such a man if he ran into them? How would he act? What would he do? They were the heirs to the legendary Fleischmann empire, Julius III or Julius IV, Caesars all, the latest lords over what today would be billions of dollars of assets. People like that probably ate people like Ben for lunch. Ben could not just drive up to their house, ring the doorbell, and start chatting with them like he was their neighbor. Some things were just not done. Some things *could* not be done. And yet that was precisely what Ben was planning to do.

"This has to be the answer," Ben told himself. "It only makes sense." After all, it was a Fleischmann who first exposed his problems at work and it should be a

Fleischmann who finally solves them. Balance, poetic justice, karma, fate—they were all on Ben's side—not to mention logic. Phil could not have paid for all those repairs by himself. And what car rental company used Equuses? No, there had to be a connection here. Phil had to be related to Julius Fleischmann somehow, and that meant money in the bank for Ben.

And so Ben decided to face his fears and approach the latest Julius about a contract with DigitALL. It would be like selling fruit baskets to Mrs. Bergen back in eighth grade, he told himself, and then he visualized how it would go. He would just need to mention that Phil and he were good buddies, watch for a reaction, and then play along, dazzling them with facts and figures. Maintaining your own computer inventory and managing your own network just did not make sense any more. Technology changed too quickly. In-house people could not keep up. It all needed to be placed gently in the hands of contractors, experts, specialists—the kind of people DigitALL had working for them.

It would be an easy sell. Surely a Fleischmann would see this. Besides, as Ben repeated his old sales mantra, "I can sell computers to cavemen. I can sell networks to Neanderthals. I can sell anything to anyone. I'm the MAN. I'm the super salesMAN." Ben pumped his fist and honked his horn, and for about thirty-five miles Ben actually believed he could do it.

However, the closer he got to Cincinnati, the more his faith in himself faltered and the grandmotherly image of Mrs. Bergen that he had held tenaciously in his mind gradually faded into a picture of a stern businessman holding a riding crop, tapping it impatiently against his leg, ready to slap him with it at any moment. No, it would take more than personal charm and a few bits of data to sell a Fleischmann anything—it would take class, something Ben was less and less certain he possessed.

Unconsciously Ben started cleaning up his Lexus—stuffing away stray papers into the glove compartment and wiping off what little dust had accumulated on his dashboard as he drove. He even rolled down the windows to air it out and found a classical station on the radio to listen to—the volume up too loud.

But his efforts did little good. By the time Ben had exited I-71 onto Montgomery Road, his hands had started sweating. They turned clammy as he passed his office and then blue as he continued up on Keller, past Blome, and down the Fleischmann "driveway."

"I'm the MAN. I'm the super salesMAN," he repeated to himself, although with less ardor. He took comfort in the fact that it would all be over soon—one way or the other.

But it was not. The driveway was much longer than Ben had anticipated, but he pressed on, slowly feeling his way along the one-lane road, between trees that seemed to close in on him and occasional houses that seemed to stare at him. It was like going back in time, back when the aristocracy ruled Europe. He thought he saw peasants peeking out behind bushes and liveried servants eyeing him from caretakers' cottages and whitewashed outbuildings.

The longer he drove, the more Ben began to feel like one of Julius Fleischmann's foxes. As the woods opened up to horse paddocks and fields, he could almost hear the hunting party, now assembled, rumbling behind him, closing in on him. Without thinking, he sped up, the imaginary millionaires in hot pursuit, intent on bringing down this lower class intruder, this peasant who was now invading their realm.

Ben's imagination was getting the better of him. He looked back several times to see if horses were indeed chasing him and almost ran off the road. He considered turning around completely when he came upon the driveway to Winding Creek Stables, but he could not. His fate was fixed. His Lexus may as well have been riding on rails. There was no turning back now. He had no other option.

"I can sell computers to cavemen. I can sell networks to Neanderthals. I can sell anything to anyone. I'm the MAN. I'm the super salesMAN."

He waved to the stable hands, as they made their way around the huge complex of interconnected barns and outbuildings and smiled at the workers in front of the glistening "crystal palace" of greenhouses, but it was no use. Ben felt something slipping inside of him. He was losing his nerve. He had forgotten everything he had planned to say. All of the facts and figures he usually kept on the tip of his mind had deserted him.

He felt like Dorothy approaching the Great Oz, but this time there was no little old man behind the curtain. The frightening head was very real—and multiplying. A family of financial wizards was waiting for him, calling to him, ready to crush him into insignificance merely by their gaze.

Still, Ben drove on. There was nothing else he could do. Desperation had driven him to this. There were no other options. He felt the weight of his family's future on his shoulders, as well as the fate of his entire department. He could not turn back now. He had to go on.

And suddenly there it was—the Fleischmann house partially revealed over the trees; the points of its gray roof and several chimneys stood like grim sentinels above the foliage. Happy to respect the "Private Drive" sign, Ben followed the other road off to the left, away from the house, and came upon a large parking lot, now empty.

He pulled into the first slot he came upon, the one farthest away from the house, and got out. Ben deliberately avoided looking directly at the house and instead found himself walking parallel to it, neither moving closer nor farther away, hoping to find an unobtrusive way of approaching it. Ben ventured onto the lush, well-kept lawn area in front. He walked down an incline to a long reflecting pool at its center but could find no sign of a secret path to the house.

Ben considered how this must look to the remaining Fleischmanns—this cowardly meandering, this sneaking

The Fleischmann Estate

around from the side as he tried to work up the courage to talk to them. Surely they could see him now as they watched him from their lofty towers. Ben could feel their merciless gaze, burning him like the sun, analyzing his every move, finding him wanting in everything their Julius had valued—courage, resolve, confidence. No, this would not do. This was not the way. Ben had to face his fear, march up to the house, and confront these people directly, personally, face to face, like he had told his reps. It was the only way.

"I can sell anything to anyone. I'm the MAN. I'm the super salesMAN."

Keeping his head down, Ben climbed the hill back up to the parking lot and walked down to its other end. There he found a walkway, marked with a sign, pointing to the house proper. He then followed its asphalt surface as it snaked between some trees and turned eventually into cobblestones. He was now in the courtyard he had seen in the photo. He was sure of it—the one with all the horses and the millionaires in it.

At this point, Ben raised his eyes just enough to make sure the horses were gone and no riders remained. To his relief, he saw no one. However, to his left, there was another, smaller patio-like area with greenery around it. It looked like it led to the front door, and so, refocusing his gaze on the ground, Ben strode as confidently as he could towards it.

Ben followed the concrete path through the patio area, straight to the house, negotiated a step onto a small porch and then found himself in front of a door. Only then did he trust himself enough to look up.

The door was immense, or so it seemed to him, attached securely to the stonework that surrounded it with three very solid hinges. To him it looked like a wooden door to a bank vault. Ben took a deep breath and prepared himself for ultimate battle. Oddly enough he felt more alert, more alive than he had in months.

"I'm the MAN. I'm the super salesMAN," he repeated one last time and then knocked, three times with his knuckles.

Nothing. No response.

Ben tried again, this time using the large knocker on the door. The loud sound surprised him as it echoed hollowly throughout the house.

Again, nothing.

Ben felt a wave of both relief and humiliation pass over him. What if no one was home? What if he had gone through all this mental torture for nothing? Ben searched for a doorbell, but finding none, took the large knocker in both of his hands and pounded forcefully on the door, not once but several times.

Again, there was no response.

Ben swore. This was not right. This was not fair. He felt his plans crashing down, dashed before this closed door, their pathetic nature now only too obvious.

"No," he said out loud. "This is not possible." He moved over to the window on his right, cupping his hands, peering into it without bothering to be discreet. What did he care if anyone saw him now? He had already made a fool of himself. He had come all this way to see the latest incarnation of Julius and, by God, he was going to see him, one way or the other. Ben rapped on the windowpane but could see nothing, no light or movement inside.

Ben took a few more steps away from the door and scanned the windows above him. Again, nothing. No face looking down on him, no curtains fluttering in the breeze, no light, nothing. He tried calling out, yelling even, but his words just dissipated into the air like so much wind. No one answered.

"This is ridiculous," Ben spat. "How could no one be at home in a house like this?" He took a few steps back, off of the porch and into the patio area proper. He began scanning the part of the house in front of him, searching for signs of life. There were none. However, as he examined the house

The Fleischmann Estate

and scrutinized its attributes, he was surprised at how intimate, even small, it looked.

It was truly an impressive structure, to be sure—but more for its artistry than for its power. The stonework around the door was stunning—with the tannish stones mostly laid horizontally but, in some panels, worked in diagonally or in V-patterns, for variety. And the windows were all leaded and exquisitely made, their light granite casings augmented with small sculptures, tying in nicely with the slate roof above.

Ben took a few more steps back and began to take in the house as a whole. The L-shaped layout of the house seemed to curl around the patio—enfolding it, hiding it, protecting it, keeping it close. The roof on both sides of it sloped dramatically to just above the first floor, minimizing its great height and reinforcing this feeling of closeness. Standing there, surrounded by living things—bushes, flowers, and patches of grass—Ben felt like he was in front of a small country house, a cottage even, something very different than the citadel of power and wealth he had imagined.

Ben turned around and accidentally kicked a small stone with his heel, sending it tumbling off under a bush to the side. He followed its path with his eyes and noticed something dark and ragged in the dirt beside it. He walked over and poked at the mass with his shoe. It was an old baseball—its stitching, for the most part, rotted away and its leather twisted back on itself, unfolding outward, like a dead cabbage.

Ben picked up the old ball and squeezed it. It felt soft and squishy, almost sponge-like—more like organic tissue than an inanimate thing. "So," Ben laughed to himself. "The barons of business actually have hearts?" It was a thought that Ben had not entertained previously. He had always pictured the Fleischmanns out with their millionaire cronies—cutting deals, attending board meetings, scrutinizing stock returns—never with their wives and children.

And yet, in this sequestered little patio, hidden in this bend of the house, Ben caught an imaginative glimpse of Julius, still in his suit and tie, playing catch with his kids—just for a moment, a precious bit of time between business meetings and social engagements—laughing with them, encouraging them, educating them, enjoying them—the way Ben sometimes played with Aaron and Amy.

Ben threw down the old ball. "No," he said. This was not the kind of Fleischmann he had come to see. He was not looking for a family man. He wanted to speak to the hyper-competent lord of this castle, the man who only thought of business. And so Ben set off to find him.

The Caretaker

> *Ironically it is often the very people considered "behind the times" regarding technology who hold the key to its success. Learning from them can ensure that the principles of communication—discovered, identified, polished and refined for thousands of years—are not lost simply because texting and e-mails seem different than verbal discussions and letters. The principles remain the same; only the form they appear in has changed.*

Ben left the patio and strode off to his right. He followed the only path he had not taken—through some trees and past another patio area into a larger, more formal garden area with a sculptured fountain in the middle. It was a beautiful place, a suitable expression of great wealth and success. Paths from this area went out in three directions spreading throughout the estate: one back to the parking lot where his Lexus was, one to yet another garden farther on, and another that followed the water flowing down from the fountain over a series of steps to a semicircular pool that sparkled in the sunlight, outlined by the dark archway that preceded it. Ben decided to follow the light.

He started down the steps, taking two at a time, eager to get to the bottom, but something stopped him midway. He paused and looked back towards the fountain's sculpture, a figure of a naked man in bronze, silhouetted against the sky—a hunter standing guard over a passel of cherubs playing obliviously at his feet.

The sculpture, as well as the way the water rippled down from its feet, seem significant to Ben somehow—and so familiar. He was sure he had seen it or something like it recently. He stopped and puzzled over the sight for a minute, and then it came to him.

This area was just like a smaller version of Ault Park, a green area in Cincinnati that he and his kids had visited just a month ago. It too had lawns and sculptures and walkways and a cascading fountain, which Amy and Aaron had great fun balancing beside, walking precariously along its edge, eager for the other to slip and fall in.

Ben smiled. He had watched them from a distance, sitting on a bench, wanting to share in their adventures but prevented by urgent duties. Despite his best efforts, there were a few emergency phone calls he had had to make and several last minute e-mails he had to send out from his Wi-Fi connected laptop. He wished that he could have played tag with them among Ault Park's gardens or rolled with them like awkward logs down its grass-covered hills, veering off in odd directions, but business interfered, as it often did, demanding that he address yet another crisis or all was lost.

Could it be that Julius felt the same way about his kids? Is that why he built this place? Not to impress his business associates but as a playground for his children? They would have loved this garden and called to him too as he sat here, begging him to come play with them. But Julius, like Ben, had pressing duties to attend to—what with running Fleischmann Yeast and all.

Obviously Julius did not have cell phones or e-mails back then, but in some ways that made his situation even worse. He would have had to explain to his family why he was leaving them, going off to the house to take an urgent call or downtown for an unexpected meeting. His children would have undoubtedly protested, but Julius, like Ben, could only shake his head no, block out their cries as best he could, and go off to do his duty.

It simply was not possible to explain to children in any suitable way why their parents could not play with them. They were simply unable at this point in their lives to see the precariousness of their situation—how the flow of capital, upon which their lives depend, could so easily be reduced or even turned off, like the water coming out of this fountain. A single mistake or lapse of judgment could be catastrophic. Success in business required constant care and an unblinking vigilance or all was lost—everything, not just their toys and niceties but their necessities as well—even the very home they lived in.

Perhaps Julius was vulnerable after all. Perhaps he saw himself more as a protector than a predator. Perhaps he was like this statue—his children's only hope—and his hope was, like Ben, one day, when they were safely grown and on their own, that they would realize what he had done for them and thank him for it.

Ben saluted the bronze Julius that stood guard above this place and continued down the steps, noting the fragile beauty of the rippling water beside him as well as the scratches on the side that, to him, were proof that Fleischman children once played there. Yes, he very much wanted to meet Julius' descendants if only to shake their hands. The Fleischmanns were fast becoming his heroes.

Ben ducked as he entered the archway, although it was tall enough to accommodate his height. It too was made of stone like the main house and its edges were rough and ragged with moss and other plant life. He squinted as he looked ahead. Beyond the archwy was the pool into which the fountain flowed. Beyond that was a wide field, stretching out seemingly for miles, the ultimate backyard. Ben found some steps to his right and climbed down out of the dark onto a bright concrete pad that extended out in front of the pool.

"May I help you?"

Startled, Ben turned around to find an old man in a khaki jumpsuit at his side, pointing the handle of a push broom at him like a spear. Ben instinctively held his hands up in surrender and backed away, stumbling over the last step.

"Sorry, I, uh, well..." Ben recovered his balance and then straightened up to his full height. "I was looking for

Juli ... I mean, Mr. Fleischmann. Do you know where I might find him?"

"Mr. Fleischmann, eh? What do you want with him?" The old man eyeing him cautiously, his hands still gripping the broom firmly, shaking it every once in a while, seemingly threatening Ben with it.

However, as Ben stood there, not knowing what to say, he looked the old man over carefully and saw how really ancient and frail he was. He was at least in his seventies, so skinny that the loose skin on his face hung in folds, like wet laundry thrown carelessly on a line. Any fear he experienced left him entirely and embarrassment replaced it. He felt silly for being startled by such an impotent skeleton. Ben lowered his hands and stepped forward a bit, deliberately trying to intimidate the man physically.

"I need to transact some business with Mr. Fleischmann," Ben said slowly, loudly, enunciating his words carefully. "I want to sell him some com-put-ers. He'll know what I am talking about."

But the old man was not intimidated. He retracted his broom from attack position. However he did not put it away. He just folded it within his arms and smiled wryly. "And an old buzzard like me will not? Is that what you're saying?"

"Basically," Ben responded, backing off neither rhetorically nor physically. He had not really meant to insult the old man. He just did not care about him enough to expend any effort to be polite. Ben just wanted to see Julius' heir and was frustrated by all the impediments he had encountered, including this man.

The old man just shook his head and chuckled. "Not very good with people, are you?"

"Look," Ben continued. "I am sure you are capable of understanding everything there is to know about Internet Protocol addresses and virtual private networks as well as PPTP, L2TP, IPsec, and SOCKS if I had the time to explain it all to you. But I don't. I'm in a hurry. I need to talk to him as soon as possible. This is an emergency. So if it is not too

THE CARETAKER

much trouble, would you please just tell me where Mr. Fleischmann is and I will get out of your hair."

But the old man didn't budge. He brushed back the few remaining strands of white hair on his head and stood there, smiling slightly, sizing Ben up. Finally he said something.

"That's okay, son. I understand," the old man replied, matter-of-factly. "I'm not offended. Some people are just handicapped socially. They don't know any better. Let me guess, you live alone—no wife, no kids—and all you do all day is sit at your com-put-er and do tech-ni-cal stuff all day long, by yourself. Am I right?"

Ben had had enough. "Fine. I'll find him myself," and with that he stormed off, vaguely in the direction of a small building he had seen over on his left. On top of everything else he had to do, he had no patience for some senile old janitor who liked to play mind games with people.

"He's not at the tea house," the old man said to the air.

Ben stopped, turned towards the old man, stared at him for a moment, and then pointed questioningly back toward the garden where he had come from.

"Nope."

Ben pointed towards the house.

"Wrong again."

Ben turned toward the field. "Out there?"

"Nope. Not there either."

"Okay, fine," Ben said, reaching for his wallet and pulling out a twenty. "Here. Is this what you want? Now, tell me where Mr. Fleischmann is, please"

The old man brushed aside the bill. "Oh, I don't want your money. I have enough of that. I was just passing the time, making conversation—you know, enjoying the day. A man can't work all the time. A man needs his breaks sometimes or it deforms him inside. Like this cow, I saw once. It ..."

Ben rolled his eyes and again turned to go. He no longer feared the Fleischmanns, but the vision he had of Julius as a supremely dedicated and efficient businessmen still haunted him and made him less patient, less tolerant

179

with delays—especially ones that seemed silly. However, the old man grabbed his arm and stopped him. He was surprisingly strong for his age and weight.

"I'm sorry. I joke around too much, I know, and I talk too much too. It's a fault—at least that's what my wife says. I'll tell you where Mr. Fleischmann is. But first I need to know your name."

Ben and the old man just stood there looking at each other.

The old man pulled Ben close and whispered in his ear. "This is where you offer me your name without my directly asking you. It's a way of showing how cooperative and perceptive you are. It indicates that we are becoming friends."

"Ben Rosen," Ben said flatly. He was not interested in becoming friends with this man.

"Excellent. You can call me Eli."

"Eli? Eli who?" Ben asked, thinking that his surname would better identify him to his superiors when Ben reported him. However, the old man either suspected what Ben was up to or did not hear him. In any case, he continued with what he was saying without supplying the requested information.

"Okay, introductions are over. We are almost ready now. However, before I tell you where Mr. Fleischmann is, I need to explain how he came to be where he is and, sorry, but this might take a while. So if you make yourself comfortable, I will proceed."

Ben groaned inside. Not more chit-chat. Still, walking around was not getting him anywhere and bribing Eli had not worked. So, perhaps the most efficient thing to do was to actually listen to the old man and hear what he had to say. Who knows? Perhaps some bit of information might actually be helpful.

And so Ben found a clean spot on the steps he had just used and sat down, bracing himself manfully for the coming ordeal. And so, with Ben properly situated, the old man began relating the decades-long history of the house, the farm, and the Fleischmann family from the 1920s until now—as he had experienced it, with as much embellishment and homespun artistry as the old man could muster.

The story, at first, was familiar to Ben. He had learned from his Internet search much of the basic outline of the Fleischmann rise to fame and financial glory. What he did not know were the details, especially about the estate and how it functioned. On this topic, Eli was truly enlightening, not only hitting the high points of its official history but filling in a lot of gaps with additional details, vivid descriptions, personal impressions, and precise directions as to where things were and what they were once used for.

Sitting where he was and having wandered about the place, Ben had no trouble visualizing its day-to-day operation and, in the process, expanded and deepened his previous impression of Julius as a responsible businessman who loved and valued his family but had little time to be with them.

But there was more. There was something in the sound of Eli's voice and the way he expressed himself—sometimes awkwardly, sometimes poetically—that not only helped Ben see the Fleischmanns in this light but to come to love and respect them as Eli had. He felt his pain as the grandeur and the glory of the estate and the family who owned it eventually faded—leaving Eli alone, the last servant of a the once thriving household now extinct.

"So the Fleischmanns are all gone? They no longer own Winding Creek Farm?"

"Yep, that's right. Julius died back in '68, and Doretta passed in '76. But the Fleischmanns had moved out of this place long before that. It was in pretty bad shape before the Cincinnati Preservation Association took it over. The Association owns most of the estate now. You probably saw the signs when you drove in—for the 'Equine Center,' the 'Garden Education Facility.' They've turned the whole place into an educational center and the house is an official historical site. They send people through on occasion on tours and hold cultural events here too—dances and concerts and such. But it's not very busy. Not much for me to clean up. I think they mostly keep me on as a kind of visual aid, a living artifact of a bygone era."

"I'm sorry, Eli," Ben said, somehow weakened by the story, content now just to sit and talk, no longer eager to go anywhere or do anything. What was there to do anyway? All was lost—not just the Fleischmann fortune but also all the business opportunities he thought to get from it. Gray clouds had rolled in, appropriately darkening the day.

"I'm sorry about your computers, Ben. I'll bet Mr. Fleischmann, if he were still alive and still owned the yeast company, would have been very interested, even enthusiastic. He was always interested in new things, new techniques. Look at the greenhouse someday. It was very advanced for its time."

"Thanks. I'll think about it."

"And I think Mr. Fleischmann would have been very interested in you, too. It took a lot of courage to come here and do what you did, and Mr. Fleischmann always admired people with courage and initiative. 'Pluck,' he called it."

"Yeah, I would have been very interested in him too—and in selling him something, lots and lots of something, anything."

The two men laughed. They were walking now. They were slowly making their way behind the house, drifting beside the stream that flowed out of the pool along a large conduit, almost an artificial creek. Up above the stream, bordering it, was a high wall, part of the structure the archway was built into. It was also made of stone, about twice Ben's height, and formed a thick barrier between the gardens above and the field they were walking on below.

Together the stream and the wall reminded Ben of a medieval moat and a fortified perimeter surrounding a castle. Behind it, the house loomed, like a citadel, a fortress of massive proportions. Here, on the back side, its roof came down only to the second floor—that and the fact that the land the house was built upon sloped away on this side, exposing its lowest level, seemed to reveal the full immensity of the place, unobstructed by trees or odd architectural angles.

It was a truly impressive structure. However, after what Eli had just told him, to Ben it was no longer a symbol of strength. It was instead an empty shell, a ruin, a restored ruin, but still a ruin nonetheless. It no longer protected the Fleischmann family or their descendants. They were all dead or scattered, exiled remnants of a once famed line. Its defenses had long been breached and its retainers defeated, leaving only Eli to tell its sad story.

In the end, Julius' approach had failed. His complete and utter devotion to his work had not been enough. All of his immense wealth and property had not been enough to keep his family together and safe. The foxes had finally overrun the place and were massing to do the same to Ben and his family as well.

"So what are you going to do?" Eli asked, still carrying his broom on his shoulder.

"I'm not sure. The quarter is almost up, and I don't have many options left. This was my only hope." Ben sighed but mustered enough energy for one last weak joke. "Are you sure all the Fleischmanns are dead? I would sure love to sell them some computer services? I can make them a great deal."

"You mean, com-put-er services?"

"Yeah," Ben said, "com-put-er services." They laughed again. But then Eli stopped, put his broom down, and scratched his head.

"Actually, I never said they were all dead—just gone. In fact there is a grandson of Mr. Julius who lives in Milford, I think, or used to anyway. Not really close to his grandparents but he used to come by some as a kid and ride the horses and swim in the pool."

"What was his name?" Ben said, doing his best not to get too excited.

"I don't remember, but he had some connection to the Association when they first started restoring the house.

What was it? No, I don't remember. Too much time. Too many things to remember. Still he was involved somehow."

"Did he have a truck? A red truck?"

"No ... well, maybe. Yes, there was a truck. I don't remember what color it was, but it had a large white sign on the door. It was the name of his company. Rejuvenation? Renovation? Resuscitation?"

"Restoration?"

"Yes, that was it. And that makes sense too since that is what the Association was doing back then. They made a big deal about it not being a remodeling job or otherwise implying that they were changing anything, although, of course, they did.

"Anything else? The full name of the company?"

"I don't remember the rest of the name. There were some initials in it, but as I recall they never made any sense to me. I could never figure out what they referred to. And the company was based in Milford. I remember that. I remember thinking that it was odd that a restoration company was so close and Milford of all places. I'd have thought that ..."

But Eli never did finish his thought. Ben hugged the old man in the middle of it, so hard that he dropped his broom.

"Thank you, Eli. You may have saved my life." And with that Ben was racing up the stone steps in back of the house, through an archway that separated the garage from the house proper, and soon he was in his car and on the phone with Bobbi.

"Hi, Bobbi? I think I've found Phil."

Phil Again

> *With oceans of facts, figures, and data now at our fingertips, technology can be extremely helpful. With it we can communicate instantly across continents and cultures. However, all this power must be handled carefully and knowledgeably.*

It did not take Bobbi long to find what Ben was looking for. She just entered "restoration," "Milford," and "Fleischmann" in Google Search. In a matter of seconds there it was: "E.F. Restoration, LTD," a private company located in Milford and owned by a Fleischmann. There was even an address and a phone number.

"Do you want me to call them for you?" she asked.

"No, I want to talk to them personally—just like I tell our reps to do."

"Good idea, Boss. Oh, this is so exciting. Who would have thought that wrecking your car could lead to a major sale. And, boy, do we need it. The rest of the reports just came in and they were disappointing."

Ben sighed. "Well, maybe I should suggest this approach to the reps. Maybe all we need is to have them 'run into' more potential clients."

"Yeah, you would bill it as an extension of the Face2Face idea. Call it Bumper2Bumper."

Ben laughed. "You're a riot, Bobbi. And such a help. Thank you."

"I try," she replied. "Oh, and your wife called. She was having trouble getting through to your cell and wondered if it was still working—at least she doesn't get an answer and no one calls back. I just thought you should know."

"Thanks, Bobbi. I'll call her."

But Ben didn't. Instead he continued down Blome, crossed Camargo near the railroad tracks, and made his way up the hill on Drake. Who would have thought that a Fleischmann company would be so close, maybe ten miles away from the office? Ben could feel excitement building inside of him. There was still hope. There was still a way to save the department, to save his job. Miracles still happened, and this one was oh so close by.

The address was as modest as the company. According to what Bobbi had discovered, E.F. Restoration had only one employee and had an annual income well below $100,000. But this was probably a one-shot deal, a front thrown together so that Phil could supervise the work on his ancestral home without attracting attention.

Perhaps in this way, Phil was continuing Julius' dream—just not at Winding Creek Farm. Perhaps he was still wealthy and well connected, but he was simply lying low to avoid notoriety and to protect his kids. Perhaps he was using disguise the same way Julius had used size—shielding his loved ones with smallness rather than bigness.

If so, that would also explain why Phil drove around in a beat-up truck and why his company did not have Fleischmann in its name. Undoubtedly the "F" stood for Fleischmann, and the "E" probably represented his middle name. But Ben could not figure out why Phil had left off the "L," but then fame does strange things to people. Maybe this was just another level of his personal security system.

Ben passed Indian Hill High School and was nearing the intersection with Shawnee Run, preparing to turn left, when his phone buzzed. Ben considered ignoring it, thinking it was just another annoying call from Sarah, but then he saw that it was Bobbi and he pulled into the Indian Hill Rangers' parking lot to answer it.

"More good news?"

"Not exactly," Bobbi's voice seemed strained somehow, uncomfortable.

"What is it? Is the address wrong? Is the company defunct?"

"No, no. Everything's all right with the company. It's the owner."

"What about the owner?"

"Well, for one I don't think he's Phil. In fact I don't think Phil is related to the yeast Fleischmanns at all."

"What do you mean?" Ben said, instantly defensive. "The company name matches, more or less, and the age is right. So what if the name is different. Phil is a nickname. This could be another way of keeping his connection to the Fleischmanns secret."

"That's not it."

"Well, what then?"

"First of all, before I tell you I need to know if you are still driving. Are you?"

"No."

"Parked or just idling?"

"Parked. Why? What's going on?"

Bobbi then proceeded to tell Ben how she had continued her research, widening her search parameters, allowing for mistypings and misspellings, investigating every hit she came upon, and in the process she discovered the real Phil.

"Okay, who is he?"

"He's a police officer—or at least, he was—and a very good one too. Let me read: 'Lamont Eugene "Phil" Fleischmann worked for Miami Township Police Department and had recently been promoted to lieutenant. He was notable for introducing cell phones into undercover police work and for initiating a program where off-duty policemen could be called up for emergencies also with cell phones.' This was back in the mid-90s. I guess cell phones were still kinda new then."

"Got it," Ben responded. "Continue."

"Okay. Well, he was helping with one of those emergencies, something to do with an alleged intruder on school property, when … You're still parked, right?"

"Yes."

187

"Okay, I will just read it to you: 'According to Lt. Fleischmann it was dark and rainy, and his wife, Helen Fleischmann, had gotten lost on her way back from a soccer match in which her children were involved. She called him for directions and he was giving them to her via cell phone when she attempted a turn going too fast for the conditions at the time. She lost control of the minivan she was driving, and it slammed into a tree. Two of the Fleischmann boys, Andrew and Xavier, were killed instantly. The third, William, and Mrs. Fleischmann were still alive when an ambulance arrived. However, Mrs. Fleischmann died en route to the hospital. William, as of this writing, remains in critical condition at Bethesda North but is expected to recover.'"

"Oh no," Ben sighed.

"I know," Bobbi agreed. "But it gets worse."

"How could it get worse?"

"Let me read on. No, I can't. I had to piece this together from several newspaper articles. The upshot is that Phil left the force soon after the accident and tried to commit suicide. He was then institutionalized for several months and his son was taken from him and given to his grandparents to raise. After that, Phil pretty much falls off the map. I found notices of fundraisers and such sponsored by the Miami Township Police Department for him but nothing else. No record of his ever being rehired or working anywhere else or going to school. It sounds like he basically became a drifter."

"Which is what he was when I met him."

"Right."

"Poor man."

"And another thing, he was not that old either. He was about your age when all this happened. But you said he looked like he was nearly 80."

"He did."

"This whole thing must have aged him 20 years. It's just so horrible. It's like Sarah and the kids dying while you were talking to them. I just can't imagine that."

"Neither can I," Ben said flatly, seemingly emotionless as he stared at the cars approach the intersection ahead of him, stop, and take turns making their way through it. The process seemed so orderly, so common-place, so automatic, and yet one little misstep on the part of one of them could result in a terrible disaster.

"Poor Phil must be riddled with guilt. No wonder he hates cell phones and talked to you the way he did. He was trying to save you. Don't you think? Rescue you from the same fate?"

Ben nodded his head yes, forgetting that he was talking on a phone.

"Oh and there's another thing. Do you know where the accident happened?"

"Where mine did?"

"Yep. Right at the corner of Ward's Corner Road and Loveland-Miamiville. The very same place. You probably parked next to the tree that killed them."

Suddenly Ben snapped out of his funk, all thoughts of selling long since gone from his mind. "Listen, Bobbi, I have something I need to do. Do you mind covering for me? There's nothing urgent that requires my attention at the office, is there?"

"No sir. Not now. At least nothing I can't handle. I'm just here to help, remember?"

"I remember. Oh and I may be out the rest of the day."

"I understand. Good luck, Boss ... and tell Phil I'm sorry."

Ben smiled. "Thank you, Bobbi. I will."

Sorry, I Have to Take This

Miamiville Again

Make no mistake, ungoverned technology is dangerous. Separated from human sense and sensibility, it can kill personal effectiveness, personal relationships, and personal happiness.

It did not take Ben long to drive to Miamiville. He turned right on Shawnee Run, followed it all the way until the T-junction with Glendale-Milford, and then took Glendale-Milford until it crossed the Little Miami River and ended at Miamiville. Ben then took a quick left and then a right back to the site of his wreck, parked his Lexus, and got out.

The area looked a little neater than he remembered it. Someone had cleaned up all the glass and cut down much of the brush on the side of the road. Phil's signs stood out prominently now. Ben walked over to them, this time noting the correspondence between the initials and the names of Ben's wife and children. He read again the words, this time with reverence, seeing in them not so much the abstract ideas from a long-dead philosopher as messages from a tormented man.

He also noticed a new sign, in the back, that had probably been covered over by the thick undergrowth. It read: "There is no more fatal blunderer than he who consumes the greater part of his life getting his living – XEF." It was for Xavier, one of the twins. Yes, it was pretty clear now. Phil was using quotations from Thoreau to apologize to his family, to somehow atone for the crime he felt he had committed against them.

Ben doubled over, overcome by Phil's pain and the pain he too felt as he pictured this same tragedy happening to him and his family. What if he had lost Amy and Aaron and Sarah in a similar way? What if he was left, like Julius, with an empty house and gardens entirely bereft of their chatter and noise and play?

Ms. Namath was right. He had allowed his work, little by little, to encroach upon his home life. He had brought in invaders—disguised as technological devices—to distort and warp his view of what he was really up to, increasing his professional anxiety until it was almost all consuming, until it took over everything.

Ben reached out to a nearby tree to steady himself. A shock went through his arm as he touched it. He looked up. The place he had touched was stripped of its bark, a naked piece of wood, about the size of a window, deeply gashed, splintered in spots, entirely at odds with the living bark that surrounded it.

Ben recoiled at once, retracting his hand out of reflex, almost falling. It was the same tree Helen had hit. It was huge and menacing, but also strangely sad too, its limbs twisted and gnarled. Ben stared at the tree uncomprehendingly, feeling somehow the tragedy of it all, deeply imbedded in its roots and branches.

"So you know?"

Ben turned and saw Phil, still wearing his plaid flannel shirt, walking towards him. Something about his steady gait and the way he held his head up despite it all made him seem less crazy, more admirable, than before.

Ben nodded. "Yes."

"Who told you? Van?"

"No."

"Billy?"

"Billy? The mechanic? No, how would he know?"

Ben stared at Phil uncomprehendingly, and then something clicked into place. "Ah, I see. He's the guy who paid for the Equus. And for the repairs too. What is he to you? An old police buddy?"

Phil smiled and sat himself up on the hood of Ben's Lexus. "He's my son. And a better son no father could ever wish for. He's a proverbial saint—and not a bad mechanic either." He patted the Lexus approvingly.

"You must be very proud," Ben said. He had not thought of Billy in a family setting before. This was something new.

"Proud?" Phil looked down at the ground and kicked at the gravel. "No. Proud would mean I had something to do with his success. I didn't. No, I abandoned him when he needed me most. I threw him to the wolves, as it were. Everything Billy accomplished he accomplished on his own, with no help from me. Even now he cleans up all the messes his worthless father makes. Why, he is more of a father to me that I am to him."

"It's not your fault, Phil. You didn't …"

"Yes, I did," Ben spat, his eyes suddenly riveted on Ben's. "I killed his mother. I killed his brothers. I killed them with neglect and ignorance and stupidity. The wreck was only the final blow. Is not my wickedness great, little man? They were already dead when they hit this tree."

Phil bent over and picked up a large stone. He raised his arm as if to throw it at the tree. But he stopped, his arm frozen in time, pain etched upon his face, his arm at the ready. And then it went limp, the stone falling helplessly to the ground.

"It's no use. It's too late for me." He turned and pointed to Ben's cell phone clipped to his belt.

"It was that thing, that beautiful, hateful thing. I bought it, I brought it into our home, I taught her how to use it, and I held it up to her head and killed her with it, in cold blood."

"Phil, it was an accident," Ben protested.

"An accident? An accident! That was no accident. Accidents happen when people fail to look both ways at an intersection or forget to put their car in park on a hill or let their foot slip off the brake at a stop sign. You hitting me was an accident. Accidents are small things—fender benders, dents in bumpers, broken headlights. This was no accident. It was murder."

Phil wiped his eyes on his flannelled sleeve. They were red and glistening. Phil was upset. That was obvious. Ben considered driving off and leaving him alone, but he could not, not yet, not after all Phil had done for him.

"I just want you to know that I've changed, Phil. I'm not the same person I was when you hit me."

Phil seemed to take no notice of Ben. "I know of no more encouraging fact than the unquestionable ability of man to elevate his life by conscious endeavor," he chanted, speaking dully, rhythmically, almost automatically, to an unheard cadence, without expression or intonation. Ben could not tell if he was actually responding to him or simply reading Billy's sign, the only one that was overtly encouraging.

"I still use a cell phone, of course," Ben continued. "I have to, but I see it now as a tool—it serves me, I do not serve it."

"Men have become the tools of their tools."

"I never use it when I drive, and I set up periods in my day when I refrain from calling people or using my computer."

"As if you could kill time without injuring eternity."

"And when I talk to people, either personally or in meetings, I put away my phone and attempt to give them my full attention."

"The greatest compliment that was ever paid me was when one asked me what I thought, and attended to my answer."

Ben continued, reporting on his progress just as Phil continued quoting Thoreau in that same robotic, monotone voice. It was as if Phil were in a trance, in a state untouched by Ben or other mortals, beyond them, for good or ill. Ben could not tell if he was getting anywhere, if he was in any way reaching Phil and letting him know that at least for Ben Phil's pain had been meaningful and done some good.

After several minutes a police cruiser pulled up and Officer Williams got out.

"Ah, there you are. I thought you might be here. Billy has been looking for you."

"Yes, I'm here. 'Not until we are lost do we begin to understand ourselves.'"

Officer Williams walked over and patted Phil on the back, stroking his arms as if to warm him.

"How is he?" he asked Ben.

"Pretty much as you see."

"Been spouting quotes from Thoreau again?"

"Yes."

"That was his wife's favorite book, you know. She was an English major. She wanted to go back to school and teach some day—in a college or high school or someplace like that. She just had not gotten around to it. Other responsibilities, I guess."

"Do what you love," Phil continued to chant. "Know your own bone; gnaw at it, bury it, unearth it, and gnaw it still."

"Good advice, Phil. Now come along. It's time to get you home to your son." Officer Williams began walking Phil over to his car, opened the passenger side door and helped him inside. After he closed the door, he turned again to Ben.

"Thanks for finding him and for calming him down. He was pretty upset this morning and took off on foot. It's his anniversary today, you know, of the accident."

"No, I didn't know."

"You're the guy he hit a few weeks ago, right?"

"Yes."

"I never forget a car. Well, then you know that Phil is usually a lot better. He has come a long way since the accident. A long way. Can you imagine hearing your wife and kids die in a car wreck?"

"No, I can't imagine it."

"I can't either. I've seen a lot of bad things during my time on the force, and this has to be the worst. Makes you appreciate your own wife and family more, doesn't it? Well, I have to get him back. Thanks again."

And with that, Officer Williams got back in his car and started it. As he drove off, Phil began yelling something at Ben. He tried to open the window but could not.

Ben was not sure, but it sounded like another quotation from Thoreau, one that he had heard long ago. "Make the most of your regrets; never smother your sorrow, but tend and cherish it till it comes to have a separate and integral interest. To regret deeply is to live afresh."

In a matter of minutes, Ben was home, talking to Sarah.

Sarah's Suggestions

As far as real communication goes, nothing can replace the sound of a human voice, the look of a human face, and the touch of a human hand—especially when they are responding to another human voice, face, and hand. All other forms of communication are compromises—situations we put up with because of distance, time, or effort. These can suffice for a time; but make no mistake, they are a lesser form.

After playing freeze tag through the gardens, Frisbee on the lawn, and racing up the central pavilion, desperately attempting to be the first to lay claim to all of Ault Park for Family Rosen, Ben felt that he deserved a rest. He leaned over the concrete railing that surrounded the pavilion's roof and surveyed his new dominion—watching his kids make their way up and then down the large cascade fountain below them.

Sarah followed suit, taking a place beside him. After a few minutes, she took Ben's hand and stroked it. "Thank you, Ben."

"For what?"

"For this day, for being you, and for saying what you said last night. I can't tell you how much that meant to me."

Ben put his free hand on hers. "I meant it, too. I've been such a fool, Sarah. I let things get to me. I allowed my concerns at work to control me, to take me away from you and the kids—even from myself. And when I found out about Phil's family, how they had been killed in that horrible wreck, and saw the agony Phil was in, all I could think about was you and the kids and how horrible it would be to lose you. And then I realized that I was already on my way. I was following the same course Phil had been on and

I knew I had to change. So, I'm sorry it took a car wreck—no, two car wrecks to wake me up. I just didn't know. I didn't know. But I'm going to change things from now on, you'll see."

Ben looked up at Sarah. Her expression was soft, thoughtful. She seemed pleased.

"I know you will, Ben. That's the kind of guy you are, the kind of guy I married. We all make mistakes sometimes. The trick is to learn from them and move on."

And so they stood there for several minutes, leaning over the railing, watching their kids, holding hands—just drinking in the joy of the moment. And then something occurred to Ben.

"Did you make a mistake, Sarah?"

Sarah looked away, brushing aside her hair, no longer confined to a pony tail, as it fell over her face. "What do you think?"

"Look, I'm sorry for being so suspicious. It was small of me. You and Derrick are just two professionals working together. I trust you to know how to handle yourselves." Ben was thinking about him and Bobbi. Sure there was a connection there—even an attraction early on—but he had worked it out just as Sarah had undoubtedly worked things out with Derrick.

Sarah brushed her hair back over her ear, but continued looking off somewhere distant, away from him. "No, you were right to be suspicious. Derrick did have other things on his mind, and I was more vulnerable than I thought."

"What do you mean?" Ben leaned forward, vainly attempting to see her face full on. "Did he come on to you?"

"No, not physically."

"Then how?"

"Well, while you were gone, he asked me to run away with him."

Ben went silent and studied the ground under his feet.

"I didn't go, Ben."

The obviousness and the earnestness of this statement broke the tension and made them both laugh.

SARAH'S SUGGESTIONS

"Of course, you didn't." Ben held her close. "You're with me, now, here, in Ault Park, and not in the Bahamas or some other exotic place. Where did he want to take you anyway?"

"Goshen."

Ben pulled away and snickered. "I can see why you didn't go with him. Goshen? Are you serious?"

"Yep, his family has a farm house there. He proposed that we move in there and work the place together and make videos on the side."

Ben laughed again. "He obviously didn't know how much you hate gardening, did he?"

"Nope." She was smiling broadly, delighting in the absurdity of the thing, and then she went serious again. "But despite all that, I found myself entertaining his offer."

"You did? Why?"

"That's what I asked myself. I thought about the kids, our house, and all the good times we had had together. I had so much to lose and yet I was actually thinking of leaving all that. Why? It was maddening. It was stupid. It was shallow. It was immature, and yet I found myself actually wanting to go off with this meat-headed muscle man to live on a dirt farm in the country. And then I figured it out."

"What did you figure out?"

"It was the regularity of his attention."

"Regularity. So all I needed to get you was a laxative?"

Sarah pushed his face away from her playfully, but meaningfully. "Stop it. I'm trying to be serious here. I'm trying to tell you something important. Do you mind?"

"Okay, I'll be good."

"You'd better. Now where was I?"

"Regularity."

"Oh yes, that is what it came down to—the regularity of his attention. I could count on us working out together at the same time on the same days every week, and I knew that he was focused just on me and only me when we trained. It sounds kind of egotistical, but when I thought about it that is what his attraction was for me—not his wavy hair, or his

199

washboard abs, his bulging biceps, his steel-like pecs, or his …"

"I get the message, Sarah."

"Sorry, I'm just teasing. I guess this is hard for me to talk about and so I joke a bit. The whole thing seems so childish, but in the end I figured it out. It was just the fact that I could count on him being there for me at the same time every week that drew me to him."

"And that was something I was not providing."

"Exactly." Sarah took his hand and stroked it, comforting him. "That's not entirely true. You used to, especially when we were in college. It's funny—we were so busy then and had too much to do, but we always had our time, and even later when you first started at Cyncom, that was true then too. But then along came more responsibility…"

"More assignments, more stress, more worries, more things to coordinate."

"All of which had to be done from home, via cell phone or computer. I remember being so frustrated that I almost chucked the computer in our bedroom out the window once and flung your cell phone out with it as well. I started to hate it. Every time the thing rang or buzzed, it was like a needle went into my heart. It just seemed to me that you were always talking on it, always checking it, always thinking about it—even when you were talking to me, facing me. It was what really mattered to you, not me."

Ben gripped Sarah's hand tighter. "I'm so sorry. I didn't know what I was doing."

"Yes, but at least you were beginning to figure it out."

"What do you mean?"

Sarah pulled her hand away from his, and looked away. "There is something else I haven't told you."

"What?"

"I was so sure you cared for Bobbi more than me—undoubtedly a projection of my feelings for Derrick—that I started going through your files on your laptop."

"You what?"

"I know, I know. But I was desperate and a little crazy. I'm sorry, but I had to know."

"But how did you get my password?"

Sarah laughed. "With a password like 'LEXUS,' it's not hard. Actually I have been using it for weeks, ever since we got the virus on the other computer."

"You have?"

"Yeah. It's back, by the way."

Ben scratched his head. "Sorry, I should have fixed it better."

"That's okay. Because of the virus I discovered something wonderful."

"What?"

"I discovered how dependent upon technology I was becoming and I saw that you were seeing the same thing."

"I was?"

"Yes, it was clear in your rules."

"My 'Rules to Avoid Being Distracted by Technology?'"

"That's right. When I saw those rules, I could see that you were beginning to understand the problem, and I had faith that you would eventually see how these things affected us and would change."

"So that's why you didn't run off with Derrick?"

"Pretty much. Remember I was desperate, I was confused, I was a little crazy. I love you and think so highly of you, but I still needed some reassurance, some hope, that things would work out, and your rules and especially the way you worked on them provided that for me. Sorry."

"So, if you had not come across those rules, you actually might have run off with Derrick."

"Well, I guess so. Yes."

"Well, it's a good thing my password was so easy to guess."

"Yes, it was."

Ben and Sarah sat there on the bench, silent for several seconds, and then, almost on cue, they turned to each other and kissed—apologizing again, and again expressing their love and faith and hope for each other and their marriage.

Then they stopped and went back to looking at the kids, enjoying the warmth of the sun, the brightness of the day, and the hint of autumn in the air. As far as Ben was concerned everything was back to normal now, settled.

"So what are we going to do now?" Sarah asked.

"What do you mean?"

"I mean, I really like what you said last night and all that, but I think we should formalize this into rules, like you did for work."

"You're kidding."

"Nope. Remember I'm an elementary school teacher. I like rules. I like order. They are my friends, and I liked the list you put together. In fact, I started using it myself."

"You did?"

Sarah looked at him as if her face made her point so well that she did not need to say anything.

"Okay, yes, I haven't been as attentive as I should have been. I already admitted that, but I am changing, I am getting better."

"Yes, you are. Yes, I use the rules every day. I even began circulating them around the school to a few teacher-friends of mine and they've been using them too."

"Really?"

"Yes, and so we've drawn up a few tentative additional rules."

"We?"

"Yes, you didn't think they were complete, did you? I thought it was an organic list, that you were going to add to it as you progressed."

"Yes, I did," Ben groaned, never realizing that his list could be used against him. "Okay, let's hear them."

Sarah then pulled out a carefully folded piece of printer paper from her pocket. She unfolded it and looked at the paper as if to read from it but then stopped. "Well, first of all, we liked the way you grouped your rules under principles. That served to reinforce the idea behind the rules and kept them from being interpreted too narrowly."

"Thanks."

"But these rules seem to belong to another principle, something different from Focus or Concentration. One of my friends suggested we call it 'Being Real,' but I think in the end we settled on 'Authenticity.' However, it means the same thing."

"Good. I like that. In a way it goes beyond merely avoiding distractions and attending to your work in a single-minded way to being true to yourself and true to others."

"Exactly. That's what we thought. And so our first rule in this category was 'No business-related cell phone calls or emails after work hours.'"

"That's a good start, and as I mentioned last night, I will gladly try to do this, but I suspect emergencies and other situations will pop up where I have to do something after hours. This can't be a hard and fast rule. Business just is not like that anymore."

"I agree. Let me read on."

Rule 1: No business-related cell phone calls or emails after work hours. Emergency calls are permitted provided they do not occur during dinner, are made in the study, do not last for extended periods of time, and are preceded by a polite explanation.

"What's a 'polite explanation'?"

"I really hate it when you ... No, I'm not going to make this personal. This group of teachers was bothered when anyone suddenly gets a call and, without saying anything, starts talking on the phone without excusing himself or herself or bothering to explain what's going on. A simple 'I am sorry, but I have to take this call; so-and-so needs to know if I want to hire some guy' shows respect to the people you are with and preserves peace, especially if the person then goes to another place to conduct the call."

"You're right. I hate that too, especially when people do that in a restaurant or some other public place. And they always seem to yell."

"Thank you."

"Is that it?"

"No, we have one more."

> **Rule 2: No business-related cell phone calls or other work on weekends or on vacations unless previously agreed upon by the spouse. Emergency work, when agreed upon, may be done but, again, must be limited in time, distant in space, and should not interfere with planned family activities. The preferred action on weekend outings and vacations is for all cell phones to be left at home and all computer connections cut.**

"Okay, that makes sense and it provides an out for weird things that always seem to come up. This is what I was trying to do today. You noticed that I did not bring my phone or my laptop."

"I did. Thank you. And aren't we having a great time?"

"We were—until now."

"What does that mean? Isn't this helpful?"

"Yes, I was kidding. It's actually enlightening. I never realized you felt so strongly about these things."

"I do. And it's not just me. Like I said, a group of teachers at school helped put this together."

"So there are lots of frustrated women in the world."

"You have no idea," she laughed. "But it's not just women; we had some men in the group as well. They are bothered by this stuff too."

"I expect so. Go on."

"That's about it actually. Although I would like it if we could set aside one night a week as a date night just for us. It's that regularity thing again. I like knowing that we have a special time and that I can count on it."

Yes, you've mentioned that several times before, but I wasn't listening. Sorry; I now think it's a good idea. Wednesdays? Just like your folks?"

"No, Wednesdays will not work because of soccer practices. How about Fridays? It will be our way of ending the work week and starting our family time."

"Ah yes, the work week." Ben said, feeling as though a cloud had suddenly come over the day.

Sorry, I Have to Take This

Preliminaries

> *Real communication involves risk. While honest and forthright communication may cause us to lose a friend, lose a sale, or even lose a job, it may also bring these things to us as well—and to a greater degree and in greater abundance than we ever thought possible. Existing temporarily in a lie is never satisfying. It is better to live forever in the truth.*

The work week did not unfold as Ben had hoped—neither it nor the week after it. Fortunately, Jill was able to rescue the Zephyr account, but that was just about all the good news that Ben heard—no new last-minute accounts from Milwaukee, Louisville, or Chicago. Detroit actually went negative while Buffalo and Pittsburgh, although adding some small accounts, did not produce revenue to push Ben's region out in front.

And Ben did his best too—not only reminding his reps of the departmental goal, but inspiring them, coaching them, assisting them in every way he could think of to reach it. He even went so far as to go with Lisa personally to visit several prospects in Cincinnati, including both Billy and the owner of E.F. Restoration. But nothing worked. Everyone seemed impressed but wanted more time to think it all through before committing.

Still, despite all the pressure, Ben stuck to his promise to Sarah and kept his work life, for the most part, separate from his home life—no phone calls during dinner, no lengthy, late-night sessions on the computer, and no texting or checking messages while watching TV with the family. Sometimes this felt more like resignation than an affirmation of his commitment to her, but he remained faithful nonetheless and retained a hope that something would somehow come through—right up until 3 o'clock on Friday when he and Bobbi had to electronically send in what was undoubtedly his final quarterly report to Corporate.

They had come so close, too. The Midwest/Great Lakes sales region had been so much more productive than it had ever been—certainly much better than anything under its previous VP. They even managed to beat out the Southeast/Atlantic and Northeast/New England regions. However, they just couldn't overtake California/Silicon. Madeline Gomez had done it again, boosting her group's sales far beyond anything anyone had expected and leaving everyone in her dust.

As Ben expected, Mr. Shaw's office called him an hour later asking when his next sales meeting was.

"October 8th, 9 a.m.," Ben monotoned.

"Very good. Please expect Mr. Shaw to be in attendance and please reserve some time at the end of the meeting ... for an announcement."

"Thanks," Ben said, wanting to add "for the warning" but just could not. All of his training told him not to burn bridges even, as in this case, if they had been carried away in a flood of figures. Ben mumbled something about the "big guy" coming next week and went home.

Ben drove again through Indian Hill and slowed as he passed "Phil's Corner," as he had started to call the place where he had hit Phil and seen him last. Ben counted the signs again. Still just four, prominent now that someone was keeping the brush trimmed. No new sign to guide him through his latest crisis and shed some philosophic light on what he was to do. He was on his own.

"No you're not," Sarah told him, when he finally mustered the courage to tell her that no miracle had come through. "You've got me. You've got us. We'll make it. Remember, 'What lies behind us and what lies ahead of us are tiny matters compared to what lies within us.'"

Ben threw a pillow at her. "Not you too?"

"What?"

"Quoting Thoreau at me."

Sarah tossed the pillow back. "Actually, I don't think it was Thoreau. A speaker at my high school graduation said it came from Emerson, but I don't think that's right either. But it doesn't matter. It's a true saying no matter who said it. We're different people, Ben; we're better now than we were before you started this job, and I can't help but think that there are practical benefits from all this."

"Like what?"

"I don't know, Ben. Maybe you won't get fired. Maybe something will still come through. Maybe Mr. Shaw will forget. Who knows? Sometimes, you just gotta believe."

"Believe?"

During the next few days Ben tried his best to follow Sarah's advice. He worked as usual—setting up a new training schedule and planning Wednesday's staff meeting, which as promised would be a "lessons learned" session with presentations from Steve and other reps who felt they had something to share.

But in his heart he could not believe that things would work out, and so he continued to think about what he would do after he was let go. Consequently, he was not surprised to find Mr. Shaw in Bobbi's office Wednesday morning just before the staff meeting, precisely at nine.

"Morning, Ben."

"Morning, Mr. Shaw."

Mr. Shaw removed his raincoat and draped it over a chair in the corner. He had dressed down today, in keeping with the dress code of a working meeting. However, the brightness of his pink Lacoste shirt and the silliness of his golf slacks with green elephants on them somehow seemed out of place for such a dreary day. He looked out a window at the gray clouds threatening rain but not yet producing it. "I thought I would bring Seattle with me today. What do you think?"

"I think I would have preferred for Seattle to remain where it was, sir."

Mr. Shaw laughed loudly and slapped Ben on the shoulder. "Yes, I would have as well." He then turned to Bobbi and rubbed his palms together. "Well, my dear, do you have any of those wonderful Cincinnati pastries for us today?"

"Yes, sir. As Ben requested, we have a table full of them fresh from Busken's in the conference room, along with juice and coffee."

"Busken's! That's it. I *love* your Busken pastries—almost as much as I love your Graeter's ice cream and your Montgomery Ribs. Are there schnecken?"

"Of course, sir, as well as some sugar-free goodies just for you."

Mr. Shaw laughed. "Oh, so you've been talking to my wife, have you? Well, she doesn't understand my needs."

Bobbi picked up her phone and pretended to press some numbers. "Hello, HR? I'd like to report some sexual harassment. ..."

At this Mr. Shaw guffawed. "Well played, my dear. Keeping an old man in his place. Yes, well played. Once again you prove that you are much more than a pretty face—smartest admin in the entire company, I'll wager. Don't you think so, Ben?"

"Yes sir." He had winced at Mr. Shaw's mention of a wager.

"So, shall all of us appropriately respected and legally protected colleagues venture off into the conference room for some much needed repast?"

"We shall," Bobbi said, offering Mr. Shaw her arm, as a man would to his date. Mr. Shaw took it and, forgetting his new place, began leading her down the hall. Suddenly Bobbi seemed to remember something.

"Just a second, sir. I have something I need to explain to Ben about the meeting agenda."

"Oh the meeting will take care of itself. They always do. Come along, my dear, schnecken can't wait." And with that, Mr. Shaw, in a way only a very old gentleman could, gently but firmly pulled Bobbi out of the office and into the hall.

Unable to resist, Bobbi twisted around while still in Mr. Shaw's grasp and pointed with her free hand to something on her desk, mouthing something like "docs."

Ben scanned Bobbi's desk. He could see lots of "documents" on it, mostly last month's status reports and requests for reimbursement. To the side was a large white cardboard box the pastries had come in—as well as her purse, keys, and what looked like a prescription from Walgreens. Nothing unusual. Ben rummaged through the stack of papers and found a draft of the meeting's agenda.

Again, Ben could see nothing out of the ordinary in this draft. There at the bottom was still the item he most dreaded: "Comments from Mr. Shaw." Ben looked outside and into the parking lot. His Lexus was only a few feet away. He could be down the stairs and out the door in a matter of seconds, and he would not have to endure the slow torture of seemingly endless PowerPoint presentations each designed to outdo the other according to the number of the rep's accomplishments and the grandness of his or her plans.

Such behavior was to be expected. They were in sales, after all. It was a competitive business where one had to promote oneself to get ahead. Still it was going to be exaggerated with Mr. Shaw there—everyone clamoring for advancement, perhaps even contending for his job.

No. Mr. Shaw would have already made up his mind by now. In fact he had probably been working on this for weeks, going over their performance reports and interviewing them over the phone. Like as not, his replacement was already in the building—one of his own reps even. Sean maybe or Steve. Both of them had been acting strangely after his visits—calling him up frequently, chatting about the department, asking him how he was feeling about its performance and theirs.

Ben examined the agenda again. Both were presenting. Aha, a perfect opportunity to show themselves as leaders and garner support among the reps, but then Jill was also slated to present. She was clearly the most competent and most consistently productive member of the department—and in Cleveland too—and she was the last one on the agenda. Maybe Mr. Shaw and Bobbi had arranged this so as to show Jill's superiority to the other two and to establish her as his natural replacement.

If Jill were to give an inspirational and forward-thinking pitch, one that taught everyone some way to better reach his or her goals, everyone would rally behind her. It would be like a coronation of the natural heir to the throne.

Ben thought again about his Lexus and how good it would feel to see DigitALL in his rearview mirror. He looked out the window again and saw that the rain had begun, a cold October rain, covering everything including his Lexus with an uneven sheen flowing in waves down the parking lot to the far drain.

No, he would go to the meeting. He did not want to get wet. Not today.

Another Big Meeting

> *Our lives, including our work lives, are mainly made up of relationships—not of tasks which can be completed and forgotten. The trick is to stay true to these relationships, not so much by "balancing" them as a juggler would a stack of dishes but by "fulfilling" them the way a conductor brings out the potential of each instrument in an orchestra. This requires discipline, of course, and a fair amount of self-scrutiny and self-sacrifice. However, the benefits are well worth it. Well-maintained relationships have a way of bringing out the best in us, sometimes in surprising ways.*

All of the reps were already in the conference room by the time Ben arrived. He hung back near the door mentally going over the departmental roster and checking it against those present. Most were in the back, huddled around Mr. Shaw, listening to him tell stories, laughing at his jokes, generally treating him like a visiting monarch laden with gifts.

Even Bobbi. Ben's heart sank as he saw her holding her orange juice like a cocktail, sipping it occasionally, giggling girlishly, her free hand touching Mr. Shaw's elbow ever so lightly. His funeral was to be more like a wake, where everyone celebrates his departure leaving him alone to mourn.

Ben moved to the front of the room and cleared his throat several times as a signal that he was ready to begin but to no avail. The group in the back chatted on, ignoring him, treating him as if he had already been replaced. Ben noticed that all three of the presenters clustered closest to

Shaw. Perhaps he had not yet decided. Perhaps their presentations were try-outs and he was going to decide at the end. At this point, Ben would put nothing past Mr. Shaw. At this point, everything he did was sinister.

Finally, Lateesha stuck two fingers in her mouth and whistled so loudly that no one could ignore her. "People, please. We have work to do here." Ben watched the group finally take their seats and wondered if Lateesha was the new VP. She certainly got people moving. Maybe she would be the best person to shake everyone up. He certainly was not.

Unable to muster any enthusiasm, Ben simply welcomed all those present, read the agenda to them, and took his seat. He felt like a corpse. More than anything he wished he had braved the rain and left in his car.

Not sure if that was his cue, Sean hesitated. However, Bobbi elbowed him and soon he was making his way up to the front, winking to the group and otherwise making a spectacle of himself. Ben turned on the projector and braced himself for several minutes of bragging.

However, Sean announced that he was going to do something "different" and requested Lateesha to join him. With much pomp and circumstance, he bade her sit on a throne-like chair he had prepared for her and crowned her with a huge paper "Very Important Customer" hat. Lateesha, always the ham, fanned herself and batted her eyelashes, all while claiming to have finally gotten the recognition she so richly deserved. Sean took a seat across from her and proceeded to pitch DigitALL's deluxe intranet service in a very plodding and uninteresting way.

The room went silent and Lateesha, picking up on this, ran off a series of one-liners apparently designed to save Sean from embarrassment. But still Sean droned on, pausing only to let the laughter die down and then continuing listing features like he was calling roll.

Suddenly Sean's smuggled-in phone rang and a ringtone based on Beyoncé's song "Listen" filled the air. Lateesha, still trying to rescue Sean, started dancing in her seat. Sean, however, ignored her antics—and the phone—and continuing to talk in a monotone, letting the phone ring several more times. Finally Lateesha could not take it any longer. "Sean, you best not keep Beyoncé waiting. Go ahead. Answer it. I don't mind."

Again, everyone in the room laughed—except for Sean. He just sat there, stone-faced, unmoved, entirely silent until the laughter subsided. Then, when everyone was quiet again, he said, in slow, clearly enunciated terms, "No, I don't think I will. Talking to you, ma'am, is more important to me than even a call from Beyoncé."

At this, the room fairly exploded with oohing and applause. Sean then stood up and with a smile explained that this was a great principle that Ben had taught him recently—that customers liked it when reps contacted them through various technologies, but they *loved it* when reps actually listened to them and focused more on them than on these devices. Such attention, according to Sean, could even make one of his extremely ordinary pitches extraordinary. And for that lesson he, again, thanked Ben.

Ben blushed. This completely caught him off guard and, after the applause had died down, thanked Sean for his praise but made it abundantly clear that he did not deserve it. He instead praised Sean for the ways he had found to minimize his time on the phone and on social media in order to maximize his personal contact with customers—setting up a daily priority list and following it so that he did not lose time inadvertently doing easier electronic things than actually talking to customers, setting time limits for his social media use, and allowing himself to work on these things only during a certain time period.

Steven next went up front. Without a word of explanation, he and Radhika took the seat previously occupied by Sean and Lateesha and proceeded to mime a sales call. It took a while for Ben, like everyone else, to figure out what was going on and why. However, after a few minutes it became clear to him that they were reenacting his interview with Steve, only in a customer setting.

Afterward Steve and Radhika led the group in a discussion about body language and explained how it showed interest in customers and promoted concentration on what they were saying. Again, Steve, like Sean, gave Ben the credit for opening his eyes to this profound interpersonal principle and thanked him personally.

Ben did not know how to react. Again, he disavowed any knowledge of this presentation. Ben lauded Steve instead for the way he concentrated on customers by making sure he "single-tasked" with them—not only by turning off his cell during customer visits, but by forbidding himself to answer e-mail or surf when he did call them. Steve also had a "preview" sheet that he looked at before all planned contact with customers, which helped him remember important facts about their situation and what he wanted to accomplish by talking to them. This was the pad of paper he then took notes on and added to as he met with customers.

After Steve came Jill, and Ben relaxed. This was all so unexpected. He could feel Mr. Shaw's eyes on him, undoubtedly thinking that he had set this all up to keep his job. Maybe he thought that Ben had even threatened his reps with retaliation if they did not go along with him. But now he would see that Ben had nothing to do with this. Jill would see to that. After the mess he had made of the Zephyr Corp., there was absolutely nothing good Jill could say about him.

And, as Ben expected, Jill passed out a prospectus on Zephyr Corp. and immediately started off explaining what business with it meant to DigitALL, She also explained who Ms. Namath was and pointed out many of her credentials and accomplishments. Jill then proceeded, with laser-like accuracy, to describe Ben's meeting with Ms. Namath—dwelling in particular on his lax attitude, his lame jokes, and his offhand remarks as well as Ms. Namath's very negative reaction to Ben's comment about his wife.

Another Big Meeting

At this point Ben was sure that Jill was his replacement. He could see what she was doing—under the guise of just being honest, she was undermining him and his approach and preparing the group for her and her style. And it was a sound approach—if she had the finesse to pull it off—but she was too harsh, too stark, in her approach, and she lacked, as Ben said all along, a sense for people—a relaxed way of relating to them, of suggesting more than blatantly stating her superiority.

Suddenly Jill stopped her narration and said, "Now you may think that this does not paint a very positive picture of our illustrious leader. And, in many ways, that is true. However, it should be noted that some people find me a little too formal sometimes. Some might even say I'm stiff, impersonal, overly serious, unforgiving, clinical, unfeeling …"

"Robotic" someone in the back added. A bad sign for a new manager, Ben thought. A ripple of semi-suppressed snickers filled the room.

Jill turned toward the general area where the joke had originated. "Robotic? … robotic?" She repeated the word mechanically, her eyes unfocused, her head twitching as though some circuit within her were malfunctioning.

Suddenly she slapped herself in the forehead as though to correct the tic and in doing so attached a circuit board decal to her temple. Ben gasped like everyone else, and then the room exploded in laughter. Her movement had been so unexpected and so skillful that it looked for all the world as if she had inadvertently opened up a panel in her skull, accidentally revealing her hidden android core.

Jill stood frozen in place for several seconds, seemingly confused by the reps' reaction. Then she smiled, slowly, awkwardly, as if for the first time.

"Ben's approach may have been awkward," she explained, "unprofessional, and painfully inappropriate for this client. However, I saw then what great lengths he was willing to go to teach me something I needed to know to be successful. He was trying to get me to loosen up a little and relate more to my customers in a real, personal, human way. He knew that this quality would enable me to sell more products and enjoy my work more. And, my dear human colleagues, I am here to say that that lesson was not lost on me."

Again the room filled with applause. However, Jill was not finished. "And not only was Ben willing to sacrifice his personal dignity to teach me an important lesson, but he also taught me a great deal about integrity. After our interview, Ben did not explain away or otherwise attempt to justify his actions; he simply apologized to me for them and acknowledged that they had been totally 'off base.' A few days later he handwrote a letter to Ms. Namath, similarly apologizing to her, describing the respect he had for his wife, and laying out lessons she and other women had taught him."

"It was not a professional letter," Jill pointed out. "It was not on company stationery, and he did not sign it using his company title or position. It was simply a personal note to Ms. Namath from a friend or someone who wanted to be a friend. He wrote her as one flawed human being to another in an attempt to undo the harm he had done her."

Jill summed up her presentation by saying, "Now you may feel that this letter was entirely inappropriate, as I did initially. However, Ms. Namath appreciated its honesty and openness and not only welcomed me back, but showed me his letter, called Ben a 'dear man,' and signed a rather substantial contract with us in the process. When I left her presence, Ms. Namath told me that she was looking forward to a long, friendly, and up-front business relationship between our two companies—a relationship I will very much try to honor as Ben has taught me by doing my best but also freely admitting my mistakes when my best is not good enough. Thank you."

Conclusion

In the end, we must remember that cell phones, e-mails, social networking software, and many other similar things have an important place in our lives. They can indeed enhance our efficiency not only in our business but also in other aspects of our lives. However, their roles must be sharply defined and controlled; otherwise, these digital devices will crowd out and take over other aspects of our lives that are necessary for our happiness and prosperity.

After the applause had died down, Ben made as if to stand, having no idea what he was going to say but still feeling that he had to say something. He appreciated the praise but, in the end, his efforts to teach and encourage the reps had not been enough. He had failed. They had not become the top department, and now he was going to get fired. In many ways, he wished that Mr. Shaw would just announce his departure and get it over with. He felt as if he was being eulogized while still alive. However he did not get a chance.

"And right now, Bobbi Blake has a presentation to make as well," Jill said as she retook her seat.

Ben looked back to see Bobbi leave her seat beside Mr. Shaw and walk purposefully up to the front. As she passed, she handed Ben a note. As slyly as possible, he opened the note under the table, out of everyone's sight, and read it. It said, "Sometimes virtual reality *is* better than actual reality." Ben looked up and stared at Bobbi wondering when he had told her about Billy's motto. She winked at him and then began.

"Well, as you all know, I don't normally present at these meetings. In fact, most of you know me only as Ben's administrative assistant. However, I think of myself as your assistant, too. I am, after all, the person you call when your link to the company intranet goes down or your hard-drive dies or you need help filling out some corporate reimbursement form or you can't figure out how to use PowerPoint or…"

"We get the idea, Bobbi. You don't have to list them all," Sid said with a smile, and everyone agreed. It was apparent that everyone knew how valuable Bobbi was.

"In general, I am the disseminator of information for the department—your network hub, if you will. And since I too have learned several significant lessons during the Face2Face campaign, I thought I would disseminate them to you as well."

Bobbi nodded to Radhika and Carmen, and they began passing out a sheet of paper to each rep.

"Just a few days ago, I went into Ben's office to retrieve some forms he had signed, and I noticed on his desk a very interesting document. It was simply called 'Principles.' This is the document you now have before you. You will notice that it contains several of the rules Ben has been encouraging us to follow for the last few weeks plus a few additional ones at the end."

"I am not sure why Ben has not distributed this document to us. Perhaps he was still working on it. Perhaps he was just waiting for the right time. I don't know. However, I think they are really, really profound as they are and make sense of many of the memos, policies, and personal counsel Ben has given to us lately. And so I would like to tell you about the last of these principles—using a YouTube video I hope you like."

Sid clapped his hands, Lateesha whooped, and everyone leaned forward. They liked videos. Bobbi passed out a copy of Ben's principles to everyone and then began.

The video was actually a cartoon, expertly drawn to look like a child's drawing, with quirky stick figures and

Conclusion

crayon coloring. It began with a character, Sally—a stick woman with a blue princess's hat and long, wavy hair—explaining how she loved her job, loved her coworkers, and loved making them happy. She was a secretary but she felt important at work, like royalty, like she was needed, and so put in long days there and often worked from home and on weekends just because she wanted to help.

"Is that you?" someone asked Bobbi. "Did you make this?" asked another. But Bobbi just smiled. "Quiet please."

Sally liked making everyone happy and this made her happy. Her boyfriend, Tom, a stick figure with a yellow prince's crown and glasses, however, was not happy. He looked very sad. He asked Sally to go canoeing, but she was too busy. He asked her to go to a restaurant, but she did not have time. He asked her to play tennis, but she had other things to do. Tom was frustrated.

This made Sally sad. She didn't like making Tom frustrated, but she did not know what to do. She tried to work faster but she did not seem to make any progress. There were just too many things to do. She could not get them done during regular work hours. Sally looked frazzled, and her previously wavy hair started to look kinky and messy and her princess's hat tilted off to the side. She even thought about quitting.

Then one day Sally went into her boss's office to put some reports on his desk. She noticed a piece of paper. The paper had rules written on it. Sally picked it up and looked at it. She liked the first two rules. She liked the idea of turning her cell phone off at home and never taking calls on vacation. She imagined, in a thought bubble, being alone with Tom on a desert island with one palm tree, two coconut drinks, and no worries.

However, with a wave she dismissed the bubble. It could never happen. She had too much work to do. She could not turn her cell phone off or leave her work at work. Everyone would be unhappy.

Then she read the third rule:

> **Given rules 1 and 2, it is only fair that similar strictures should apply to personal calls and e-mails during business hours. One's business life affects one's personal life and vice versa. The only way to deal justly and authentically with them both is to separate the time devoted to each in clearly demarcated ways and to prevent any digital encroachment across those boundaries. Those who divide their time in this way find their effectiveness in both of these areas improves.**

Sally looked puzzled. She scratched her wavy hair under her princess's hat. This rule did not make sense. She never called anyone or sent personal e-mails or shopped online at work.

Or did she?

Several thought bubbles suddenly popped up above Sally—one showing her talking to Wendy, her best friend, on the phone; another showing her sending her mother an e-mail with photos of her trip to Philadelphia; another of her buying a new pair of shoes online; and another of her updating her Facebook wall. Sally was shocked. Her stick figure mouth formed a large O and her hands went up to her stick figure cheeks.

Sally decided to perform an experiment. For a week she decided not to do any personal business at work. She would see if it made any difference.

And so Sally did not call any of her friends or take any of their calls while she was working. She left all of her personal emails for later and only surfed the Internet for work-oriented purposes. She never looked at places to vacation or clothes to buy or even the news. And, above all, she left Facebook and other social networking sites alone—at least until she got home.

And, voila! Sally found that she got much more work done at work. In fact she found that she did not need to work as long as she had before. She therefore had more time for Tom, and Tom, along with everyone else, was very happy.

In fact, at the end of the video, Tom, got down on his knees and proposed to Sally and as she stood there contemplating in her stick figure form what to say, she magically morphed, an amazing technological feat, into Bobbi, a real person who smiled broadly and finally said yes. THE END.

At this point, all of the women in the room screamed and mobbed Bobbi to see if it was really true. Meanwhile all the men applauded loudly and demanded to know how she put together such a great video.

"It was my fiancé," Bobbi chirped, answering both questions at once. She proudly held out her left arm, just like Sally had, averting her eyes and cocking her wrist downwards to better show off her new engagement ring.

"Yes, Tom and I are getting married in the spring," she announced, and then provided some basic details. "But don't let all this overshadow my main point," Bobbi said loudly, assertively, in an attempt to bring the room back to reality.

"It was Ben who actually allowed this to happen. Ben showed me that you can do it all—or at least most of it. You can be very effective at work and still have a life outside of work if you are disciplined and careful. Thank you, Ben, for everything. I love Tom but I also love you all and I love DigitALL. I want to make you all happy, and Ben showed me how to do it. I hope you will take all the principles to heart."

Everyone immediately looked at Ben.

Ben once again did not know what to say. On the one hand he was incredibly flattered, but he was also relieved. He still harbored a suspicion that Bobbi still had a crush on him, and all through the video he was certain that it was obvious to everyone that she was doing this just to ingratiate herself to him. But now that impression was cleared up. He was safe. Everything was resolved. Bobbi was involved with someone else, and there was no doubt about their relationship.

However, there was still the matter of Mr. Shaw. Everything else was tied up neatly. It was time now to face the real music. "I believe Mr. Shaw has an announcement for us," he said dully, and everyone turned to look at Mr. Shaw, someone they had temporarily forgotten.

"Yes, yes I sure do, as a matter of fact. I do have an announcement of my own," Mr. Shaw cleared his throat and slowly made his way to the front of the room. "Ahem, do you have the box, Bobbi?"

"No, I'll go get it. I'll be right back. Just a sec."

"Thanks. While Bobbi is retrieving the box—*my* surprise box—I want to say a few words about this meeting."

Lateesha groaned and put her head down.

"Not to worry, Lateesha. You were marvelous as a customer—and you, Sean and Steve and Radhika and Jill, were also all excellent. In fact I don't think I have been to a more productive and educational as well as entertaining sales meeting since the early days of DigitALL."

"You may have heard this story before, but I started this company with two partners—Levi Leverson and Bea Morton. Levi was a networking genius, the 'Einstein of the Ethernet,' we used to call him, and Bea could have organized D-Day in her sleep. They were great people and great workers, but they were also interested in a thousand things—astronomy, hiking, sailing, chaos theory, cards, everything. It was hard for me to rein them in. That was chiefly my role—to direct all that intellect, to control it so that it was going in a productive direction."

"Anyway, we had wars back then. Levi and Bea were so energetic and so capable, but they needed breaks, they said, or they would die—or worse, quit."

"And so we came up with a company motto, which has gone by the by, of 'Work hard and play hard.' This I thought would provide the necessary balance and would fuel both aspects of their lives while still generating the great monetary success that this company had enjoyed. And more than any other department in DigitALL, your group, Ben, has demonstrated the value of such an approach, especially considering what I saw today."

"And so I have a little surprise for you all today. Bobbi, the surprise box please."

Bobbi who had just returned to the room gave Mr. Shaw the surprise box. Mr. Shaw took the box and made as if it were heavy. He then shook it a bit. Something rattled inside.

"All right now; Ben, if you will come up here, I can make this presentation."

Ben did so, although apprehensively. This was not how he imagined being let go—with a present, a present he knew nothing about. Mr. Shaw was playing one of his games again—somehow twisting a bad thing into a good thing.

"Ben, on behalf of all of DigitALL, I present you and your department with the first annual Leverson-Morton 'Work Hard, Play Hard' award. Go ahead, don't be shy. Reach in."

Ben did so and pulled out a computer mouse in the shape of a yoyo. And everyone clapped politely.

Mr. Shaw stood there grinning until the tepid applause died down. "Oh, did I mention that there is a thousand dollar bonus to each member of the department included in this award?"

Instantly the volume and vigor of the applause increased tenfold.

Again, Mr. Shaw continued grinning long after the applause eventually died down. "Anything else in there, Ben?" he asked, knowingly.

Ben shrugged his shoulders.

"Well, go ahead and look."

This time Ben pulled the lid back and saw a trophy with a tennis player on it. He pulled it out.

"When I was in high school," Mr. Shaw said, in his best announcer's voice. "I played on the tennis team. I was not a very good athlete in general and was actually pretty bad when it came to tennis. Nevertheless, I worked hard and eventually got to play some of the lower doubles matches. At the end of the year, I was given this trophy—the Most Improved Player award."

"You all are the most improved sales department in all of the company. Last year you were the worst. You stunk, frankly. You couldn't sell a cupcake to a starving man. But this year you are number two in cumulative sales. That is an incredible achievement, and I want you to know how much I and the company appreciate your hard work."

Again there was much applause. Sid then asked if there was any money attached to this award as well.

"Funny you should ask that. There is. Here is the envelope, Ben. What does it say?"

"2K."

"That does not refer to the year this office was established. That is how much each of you gets as part of this award. Thank you again. Thank you all again. Now, let's do lunch. It's on me."

The meeting then disbanded with all the reps noisily going to Outback for a specially- arranged lunch. Each of them went by Mr. Shaw and Ben, shaking their hands and thanking them almost as if Ben's funeral had turned into his wedding. He thanked them in turn—especially Sean, Steve, and Jill.

Afterwards, when only Ben and Mr. Shaw remained, Ben thanked Mr. Shaw for praising his department and asked if he should start packing up his things now.

"Why?"

"Well, aren't you going to fire me?"

"Fire you? Get real. I'd have to be an idiot. I just gave you an award. Why would I fire an award-winning vice president?

"I don't know," Ben shrugged. "Perhaps because you told me that if my department wasn't the best department in the company by now you would."

"Oh, you mean the bet?"

"Yes, sir. The bet."

Conclusion

"Well, never mind that. Jennings finally retired two weeks ago so all bets with him are off. And a good thing it was too. His health was failing and his wife had a long list of places she wanted to visit—cruises and such—you know, so he could regain his strength and she could see the world."

"So I still have my job?"

"Why, yes, of course, if you still want it. I realize you may have made other plans, so I am prepared to offer you a sizeable increase in your salary. Naturally, it will be tied to your department's new sales goals, which will also be increased, but after what I have seen today, you should have no problem meeting them."

Mr. Shaw stuck out his hand. "So, do we have a deal?"

Ben hesitated. He should have been overjoyed. He should have been thrilled. He should have been relieved. But he was not. He had heard so much about Mr. Shaw's ruthlessness that now when mercy was offered, he did not trust it—even when it was staring at him in the flesh.

"Oh, I suppose you want stock options too, eh Ben? Well, that's smart of you. Maybe next year. You just keep advancing confidently in the direction of your dreams, and endeavor to live the life you have imagined and you will meet with a success unexpected in common hours."

Ben stopped and started at Mr. Shaw. "Did you just quote Thoreau, sir?"

Mr. Shaw looked embarrassed and turned away. "Did I? Well, I suppose I did. Sort of, anyway. I forget the exact words sometimes." He looked again at Ben. He seemed more subdued somehow, less intense.

"Henry David was my inspiration for creating this company, you know. Yeah, all that marching to different drummers, following your genius, and waking up stuff finally got to me. It pushed me over the edge and gave me the confidence to strike out on my own. I even wrote in my journal that I started this company because I wanted to work deliberately; I wanted to work deep and have a company that would put to rout all the bureaucracy and politics and silliness I had experienced to that point in my professional career. I did not want, when it came time for me to retire, to discover that I had not really applied myself, at least professionally."

Ben shook his head. "That's heady stuff, sir. I never realized …"

"What? That I had some depth to me? That I read? That I think? I do, you know—more than you imagine. My methods are not as crazy as they may seem sometimes.

"I am beginning to see that, sir."

"So will you accept my deal?"

Ben straightened up, but more out of respect than fear. "Yes, sir. I do. I do accept your deal."

"Excellent." And with that Mr. Shaw took Ben's hand and shook it vigorously. But Ben did not let go.

"And can I really have stock options next year?"

Mr. Shaw laughed. "You bet," he said with a wink. Then Ben laughed, and together they walked out of the building, across the parking lot, and into the restaurant where the others were waiting for them. Before he went in, Ben looked up. The rain clouds had all moved on and the sky was clear and blue, for now.

Epilogue

And the LORD turned the captivity of Job, when he prayed for his friends: also the LORD gave Job twice as much as he had before. (Job 42:10)

Sarah and Ben are working things out. Ben sees Phil on occasion and waves to him. Phil still harasses people who use cell phones too much. Billy is still thinking about using DigitALL's services. Ms. Namath has expanded her operations greatly and keeps Jill extremely busy. Eli gave the Rosens a tour and announced that he could be retiring soon, but no one believes him. Bobbi and Tom have set a wedding date—next June on Mackinac Island.

And Ben got to keep his job.

Sorry, I Have to Take This

Part Two: Ben's Principles

Sorry, I Have to Take This

Principle 1: Focus

Modern technology can help increase productivity, but it can also serve as a distraction from more important tasks and provide a temptation to put off such tasks. Therefore, these devices must be used in a limited, purposeful, and disciplined way.

> **Rule 1: Actually attend all meetings.** This means more than just being physically present; it means being mentally present as well—focusing exclusively on the issues at hand and bringing to bear all of your faculties on those issues. You should therefore not be typing, sending e-mails, texting, checking messages or in any way using a cell phone during a meeting. In fact, cell phones are not allowed in meetings. Focusing in this way will ensure shorter, better, and more productive meetings.
>
> **Rule 2: Don't take or make any calls while driving to work or for the first hour at the office—no appointments either.** Set the time aside to accomplish strategic activities. Ideas will come if you don't drive them away with "noise." They are like fish; they take time and patience and quiet to catch.
>
> **Rule 3: Always have a specific purpose and a time period in mind when using the Internet, especially social networking sites.** Write it down and stick to it. If you can, even set an alarm to remind you.
>
> **Rule 4: Don't check your cell phone or take calls while speaking to someone.** Not only is it rude, but also it keeps you from focusing on what that person is saying and limits your response to him or her. It

shows you are not really mentally or emotionally there for the person and indicates you would rather be somewhere else.

EXPLANATION OF THE PROBLEM

Many businesspeople struggle on a daily basis to maintain their focus in the face of modern technology. Several prefer to do easy electronic work (email, texting, checking Facebook) instead of doing strategic items such as writing a brief (attorneys), creating a presentation (speakers), setting up a meeting to terminate an employee, or dealing with a complex billing situation, etc. In essence, many businesspeople don't concentrate on completing the "hard things." This common preference is compounded by electronic devices because distraction is even more easy thanks to texting, Instant Messaging, social media, Internet news, and other electronic distractions. Frequently, people let curiosity distract them from their real priorities. Basex, which describes itself as "the world's foremost authority on the issues companies face as they enter the knowledge economy," estimates that companies lose $650 billion each year due to the "cost of unnecessary interruptions" in terms of lost productivity and innovation.[1]

Another challenging issue many people face is the decision over how to use short stints of time, as short as 15 minutes. People often choose completion of a small insignificant activity over partial work on a strategic item. Businesspeople rationalize their choice because they can actually complete the less-important item rather than just starting work on a section of a strategic item. Frequently, professionals will procrastinate those big items until they have several hours of free time to work on that difficult, complex problem.

---

[1] Steve Lahr, "Is Information Overload a $650 Billion Drag on the Economy?" *The New York Times*, 20 Dec. 2007. Web, 5 Aug. 2011.

However, the dirty little secret is that those large blocks of time rarely ever occur. In a modern business setting (other than on an airplane), it's rare to have several hours' worth of concentrated time to actually knock out a project. So, people procrastinate doing those strategic items, work on weekends to catch up on critical projects, and then lose track of their work-life balance—all because they chose checking email over doing a small section of their big task, day after day after day.

Many people think that short stints of time wasted on the Internet or on Facebook don't really matter. However, these "short stints" create big problems. Even though businesspeople frequently only spend short periods of time with digital distractions, those distractions add up. They take people away from important activities for themselves, for their family, and for their professional pursuits. Time spent with digital distractions has consequences, and the lack of meaningful activities eventually has significant negative consequences. It's similar to an individual who frequently snacks on small candy bars throughout the day and skips meals that provide real nutrition. Because of this wasted time due to digital distractions, you might miss some of the best moments in life or are so digitally distracted that you don't fully appreciate those special experiences.

Throughout my coaching work, I've met many professionals who have chaotic lives with little time for serious thinking. They seem to be constantly bombarded by email, instant messaging, text messages, Twitter, pings, and other electronic distractions. After a while, these people feel that electronic devices are controlling them and not vice versa. Because they're reacting too much to the distractions in their life, they feel stressed out and have cluttered minds. One of the symptoms of people in this situation is that they have an absence of focus. They juggle between their personal and professional lives and seem to be unsuccessful in each camp.

SELF-EVALUATION

You may not have a problem with focus, or you may be challenged by only one aspect of this general issue. To evaluate yourself, ask yourself how often you perform the following tasks, and score yourself appropriately: 1=never, 2=infrequently, 3=sometimes, 4=often, 5=always

Then proceed to the next section to learn how you can better accomplish a particular task.

	1	2	3	4	5
1. I create a daily, prioritized activity list.					
2. I accomplish hard, strategic, complicated items in the first half of the day.					
3. I set routines for the first half of the day.					
4. I frequently set aside long stretches of uninterrupted time to concentrate on and accomplish important items.					
5. I create time segments for customers, employees, and myself.					
6. I use PM appointments.					
7. I develop digital time zones.					
8. I use power hours—focus times—to accomplish strategic items.					
9. I prepare myself for small breaks so that I fully utilize short stints of time on strategic items while I'm waiting, driving, or the like.					
10. I use an accountability partner.					

Solutions

In addition to benefiting from Ben's rules, you can overcome problems with focus by following this ten-point plan.

1. Create a daily, prioritized activity list

The most important activity you can do at the end of each day is to create a prioritized list of your next day's tasks. Then, you need to gather the willpower to actually work on the first item first and so on while working down the list. If you have a clear work plan developed the night before so that you're ready for your work each morning, then you're less likely to fall into the trap of doing "easy work." If you don't have a prioritized list of daily activities, you reduce your chances for successfully completing strategic items because you'll have more uncertainty in your life. With uncertainty, you are likely to gravitate toward accomplishing easier tasks. However, if your priorities are created in advance, it's much easier to simply work off those plans. Even with these plans in place, inevitably you'll have customer/employee emergencies that come up. Because you've created a plan, you can then prioritize those customer demands into your current plan. Because of the strength of the plan, you will not just immediately rush off and respond to the customer; rather, you will decide where that customer request fits into your plan.

Keith

Keith is one of the best leaders I know. Keith has several successful habits: He's disciplined about setting up a weekly plan to make sure that he plans out his own work. He also distributes some of the work to his staff. In addition, he is a master at doing the most important items first. He typically gets to the office early, and in an uninterrupted fashion he knocks out key projects before the staff gets to the office. After the staff arrives, he is then available to manage the normal crises that arise. This habit has served him well.

2. Accomplish strategic items in the first half of day

Because the latter half of the day is typically unpredictable, an important step in improving your focus is to complete strategic items in the first half of the day. Most people have more energy and fewer emergencies in the earlier parts of the day, so it's the ideal time to complete "hard things." The choice to work on strategic items is a clear decision. As outlined in the previous step, you need to decide that your first things actually come first. For example, among Americans who maintain a regular exercise routine, 90% complete their exercise in the morning before distractions can set in.[2] Similarly, at work it's vital to do the most important items first each morning.

3. Set routines for the first half of the day

This part of the day should have a solid element of routine in it so that it can be powerful and focused. Of course, none of this works without discipline. We've all experienced times in our lives when we've had stronger and weaker routines. In my coaching, I've found that some of the most successful professionals have very robust routines while persons with more irregular schedules struggle. It's easy just to say that you'll have more discipline. It's much harder to actually implement that discipline. Greater discipline typically comes from a clear vision of the benefits of the activities, a partner who holds you accountable, and penalties/rewards for your discipline. The key is that you create this routine so that you're able to follow it and start your day with discipline.

4. Set aside time segments for concentration

After you've set up the prioritized task list with a few routines nestled in, create specific times each week when you're unavailable to others. These are time zones in which

---

[2] Lyla Feldman, "A Morning Exercise Routine - It Is Possible!" EzineArticles.com, 27 June 2008. Web, 20 Sept. 2011.

you get away from everything and can pursue creative enterprises. Mark this block of time on your schedule as appointment time so that coworkers and clients won't intrude on it. You should consider it as sacred time for innovative reflection with zero distractions (in effect, a "clean" zone). I recommend that you designate not only a time but also a quiet, *media-free* location where you won't be disturbed by customers or employees. After establishing these time segments in your schedule, check to determine that they actually fit with your body and its rhythms. It's critical that you prioritize your times zones to make sure that you're doing your most important and most difficult work during periods when you have the most energy. Additionally, you should fully understand your limits and determine the activities over which you have control and those over which you do not. Your focus-time zones should be fully in your control. They will give you a sense of liberty and motivation as you go through your day despite doing activities in which you're at the mercy of your customers, your employees, or your supervisor.

Robert

Robert is a successful attorney who knows his limitations and his abilities. One of his keys to success is to go to the library to have quiet time. There are no distractions of any kind at the library—no phone calls, no text messages, no assistants, and no anxious clients. At the library, Robert is able to plow through his work. Because of this quiet time, he has been able successfully to create his briefs and organize his thoughts. He recognizes that while he is in the office he needs to be dedicated toward serving his clients, interacting with other attorneys, and leading his staff. On the other hand, the library has become a "focus zone" for his serious thinking and deliberations.

5. Make time for customers, employees, and yourself

I also recommend that in addition to focus-time zones, you set aside time segments for strengthening your customer relationships, employee relationships, and your own skills and personal interests. In my coaching, I've found that it's very important to have your personal activities support your professional activities. When your personal activities are fulfilling and rewarding, you're in a better position to complete your work activities. For example, as I trained for three marathons, I noticed that as my training improved my business picked up. Specifically, it's important to put a variety of activities into your schedule each week: time for meditation, time for exercise, time for family, and time for relaxation. Set up boundaries (such as 6-9 p.m.) when you're completely off-line, and clients and co-workers know that you're unavailable.

Bob

Bob is the leader of a networking group, an attorney, and a principal partner in a credit repair company. He has flourished in all three ventures. A secret to his success is that he sets aside key times to accomplish strategic projects. He also realizes that these projects will take substantial time, so he schedules weekly and bi-weekly "work-at-home days" in order to be an effective leader and to stay on top of his paperwork. Thus when Bob works at the office after his strategic work is already completed, he is free to be available for clients and his leadership team.

6. Schedule afternoon appointments

As they plan their time segments, many successful professionals schedule most of their meetings in the afternoon so they can be free to do strategic items in the morning. In business, you need to accomplish both proactive and reactive items. If you complete the proactive items first, you'll be liberated to complete the reactive items later—knowing that you've completed the most important items first.

7. Set up digital time zones

In addition to establishing various time segments, it's critical that you also set up regular intervals for checking email, texting, instant messaging, etc. You won't be able to have productive focus time segments unless you're able to clearly set aside time to do these supporting activities. There is a time and a place for this "constant availability," and there's also a time and a place for less communication. In many cases, it's similar to professors who have "office hours." These time segments are for interruptions, meetings, and random activities. There is the risk that unstructured digital time will lead to distracting, time-consuming activities. Set clear boundaries for what you want to accomplish on the Internet and time limits for how quickly you'll accomplish each item. Set boundaries for the amount of time that you'll spend on social media, texting, cell phones, email, television, video games, etc. Know when you want to spend time in these areas and when you can be most productive or gain the most relaxation from these activities. In fact, I encourage people to set timers for their involvement with electronic interactions. Buy a special timer that has a snooze and a progressive bark so that you know how much time has been spent. Because they are inherently addictive, it's important to have a "wake-up alarm" to stop the addiction.

Scott

Scott is the former CEO of a successful executive recruiting firm. When asked what he did on a daily/weekly/monthly/annual basis that was critical for business success, Scott said he spent a significant amount of his time doing goal setting with his employees. He had the employees create annual goals and then translate those goals into daily activities. His approach was to move from long-term goals to focus on daily activities and take the necessary actions for success.

Scott also insisted that employees prepare their plans for the following day on the previous afternoon and then leave those plans out on their desks where they would be seen on the next day. This helped his employees start out each day fresh, ready, and totally directed. Scott would frequently walk through the office in the late evening and write helpful notes of direction on the employees' plans.

Scott gave his employees monthly reviews with written goals. During the reviews, he would scan through the daily plans with the employees (which they would compile) to look for problem and success areas. Another philosophy he followed was: "If you don't track something, you can't improve. If you're not keeping score, you can't improve." Because he targeted growth, Scott increased sales at his company by 100% every year for over a decade.

8. Establish Power hours with a partner

Many professionals struggle to have the discipline to do some of these focus time segments. One way to increase your discipline is to have regular "power hours." These power hours start and finish with a partner (typically a coworker) to motivate you and give you accountability for that time. The power hour typically consists of activities that utilize your best talents. These activities could be sales calls, writing presentations, employee reviews, connecting with customers, etc. These activities use your best gifts and are typically times when you're able to make the most impact for your company.

9. Prepare for short stints of time

The key to the full use of short stints of time is preparation to deal with tasks such as a phone call list for salespeople, key reading for a manager, or some small part of a project for an engineer. In that short quarter of an hour or so, you have a decision to check email, social media, and the news, **or** to work on a strategic item that will further your business or personal life. Without preparing in advance, you will most likely choose to do the easy task. However, if you prepare, you can utilize that time profitably to actually make a difference.

10. Employ an accountability partner

One of the best ways to focus on strategic items is to employ an accountability partner to whom you're accountable for results and timelines. Have this person know your strategic items for each day so he or she can follow up with you on the completion of those items. It's much easier to work on those items when you know that you've got to report about your activity or lack thereof.

Sorry, I Have to Take This

Principle 2: Concentration

Rule 1: First of all, figure out what your work is fundamentally and learn to devote all of your attention to it. This is especially true if your work involves people. Remember to concentrate on them and not on the tools you use to reach and to teach them. Do not be distracted from this, your primary purpose.

Rule 2: Show your interest in the people you work with by taking time to talk with them individually in a setting that promotes a sense of security and mutual respect. Make eye contact and truly listen to them, and demonstrate that you take them seriously by taking notes on what they say and by acting on their comments. They often have really good ideas.

Rule 3: Never take a phone call or even look at your phone while in conference with another person. This will seem like an emotional betrayal and will show a lack of interest in that person and in his or her ideas. In addition, as you are listening to that person, take occasional notes on what he or she is saying and consider how that person or activity helps your larger goals. Not only will that person will feel more valued and appreciated, but you will be better able to better use those ideas to further your goals. In the end, everyone gains.

Note: Cell phones are great tools for sales personnel. However, during sales calls, cell phones need to be turned off so that the salesperson can focus attention on more profitable activities such as concentrating on a prospect.

Explanation of the problem

One of the greatest problems businesspeople struggle with relates to multi-tasking or a lack of strategic focus on the task before them. This ranges from surfing the Internet while talking with an employee to texting while talking at the dinner table to playing a videogame while on a webinar. We see this abundantly in the business world where businesspeople haven't decided which activity they want to accomplish. Frequently, they're trying to accomplish two items at once while being unsuccessful at each. In addition, many professionals have bought into the myth that multi-tasking is effective. Yet it can be considered disrespectful to disregard the person with whom one is having a face-to-face conversation in order to take cell phone calls or read text messages.

In addition, there is a temptation for businesspeople to consider the **person** or **key strategic item** in front of them as being dull in comparison with the *potentially* exciting person/message/image that is embedded in their electronic device. As this continues, the people who are close by start feeling less and less important. This could be true especially for businesses that attempt to save costs by lessening face-to-face interactions and substituting those interactions with teleconferencing, webinars, and electronic communication.

Self-evaluation

Again, you may not have a problem with this principle or you may be challenged by only one aspect of this general issue. To evaluate yourself, ask yourself how often you perform the following tasks. 1=never, 2=infrequently, 3=sometimes, 4=often, 5=always. Then proceed to the next section to learn how you can better perform a particular task.

CONCENTRATION

	1	2	3	4	5
1. I believe in single-tasking.					
2. I commit to concentrate fully with an open mind and a clear purpose on each single task or person with whom I am interacting.					
3. I engage all my faculties so that I am contributing to the interest and success of the interaction.					
4. I use a partner who will help me keep my commitments.					

SOLUTIONS

In addition to Ben's rules, I recommend that you use the following four-point plan to overcome problems with concentration.

1. Believe in single-tasking

Many forces in the business world are conspiring against being able to focus well at work. The first step in focusing is to **believe** that single-tasking has merit and that multi-tasking doesn't work. The first step is for you to review the academic research and gain a complete belief in the fact that multi-tasking does not work and that multi-taskers actually do both activities poorly (see Frontline Series).[3] If you wrongly believe that your relationships and your work are positively affected by multi-tasking, then you'll never be able to overcome this problem. Altering your belief system is essential to overcoming the plague of multi-tasking.

---

[3] Nicholas Carr, "Does the Internet Make You Dumber?" *The Wall Street Journal*. Dow Jones, 5 June 2010. Web, 30 Jun. 2011.

Mike

According to *The Wall Street Journal*, Mike Periera, "a rules analyst for Fox Sports," about NFL football knows how to single task. During one of the biggest blown calls in the history of the sport, people sought out Periera's opinion on the call, but he was unavailable on a fishing trip. Despite the possible temptation to comment on the situation, his friend said about Mike, "When he was fishing, he was just fishing."[4]

2. Commit to concentrate fully on each single task/interaction

The next step is making a **commitment** to concentrate fully on each single task/interaction with an open mind and a clear purpose. With this commitment, you then have the liberty to focus 100% on the person or activity in front of you. Focusing instead on the person/activity/event on the screen is a problem for many professionals.[5] If you don't have want to commit to that activity/person, then have the integrity to not participate in that activity or to be with that person. Turn off devices each time you're with someone or doing strategic items, and avoid mixing work and play. This is a common issue among professionals who bring work issues to home and home issues to work. One strategy some of my clients use is to write out key business items before leaving work and key personal items before leaving home so that they can honestly concentrate on both areas of their lives.

Bob

Bob is a master at making people feel important. He has made a commitment to be "present" in all of his appointments. He has determined that any meeting he is in

---

[4] Gay, Jason, "How Would You Make This NFL Call?" *The Wall Street Journal*. Dow Jones, 1 Oct. 2012. Web, 1 Oct. 2012.

[5] Nicholas Carr, "Does the Internet Make You Dumber?" *The Wall Street Journal*. Dow Jones, 5 June 2010. Web, 30 Jun. 2011.

is worthwhile—and therefore should not be interrupted except for a few true emergencies. He is an expert in the power of focus.

3. Engage all your faculties

Once you believe in single tasking, your next step is to **engage** so that you're contributing to the interest and success of the interaction. Your job is to improve the current work or to show more interest in the people in front of you so that they're more interesting than the "digital distraction." You have the responsibility to engage in the process and not stand idly by watching the situation. Some strategies for focusing more on the person/task in front of you are these:

- Demonstrate your interest to people around you so that they know you're "totally with them." Do this by taking notes, giving eye contact, thinking about what they are saying, and acting on their comments.
- Make items in front of you more interesting by reflecting on how the person or activity impacts your goals. By understanding a person's importance to your goals, you'll hopefully have more motivation to be engaged with him or her.
- Keep your focus times short (typically 30-45 minutes). You can focus better by having regular intervals of unstructured time to let yourself relax, meander, and daydream so that you can be especially focused during your short stints of focus time. This relaxation strengthens your ability to focus during your productive time.
- Encourage team members to turn off their devices during meetings so that everyone is committed to the meeting.
- Imagine that each person sees exactly what you're seeing.

4. Use an accountability partner

When some professionals find the activity very important, they'll actually have a **partner** such as a coworker or coach who will help them keep their commitments. This partner gauges progress. Typically, without a partner it's almost impossible to know whether you're succeeding or failing. This partner fills the role of a guide to help you know if you're making real progress toward a focused lifestyle. If you don't have the benefit of using a partner, measure your attentiveness for your focusing abilities in the present moment. This can be done by snapping a wristband when distracted, counting interruptions, or scoring your attentiveness, etc.

Principle 3: Authenticity

Rule 1: Don't take or make any business-related cell phone calls or e-mails after work hours. Emergency calls are permitted provided they do not occur during dinner, are made in the study, do not last for extended periods of time, and are preceded by a polite explanation.

Rule 2: Don't take or make any business-related cell phone calls or other work on weekends or on vacations unless previously agreed upon by the spouse. Emergency work, when agreed upon, may be done but, again, must be limited in time, distant in space, and should not interfere with planned family activities. The preferred action on weekend outings and vacations is for all cell phones to be left at home and all computer connections cut.

Rule 3: Given rules 1 and 2, it is only fair that similar strictures should apply to personal calls and e-mails during business hours. One's business life affects one's personal life, and vice versa. The only way to deal justly and authentically with them both is to separate the time devoted to each in clearly demarcated ways and to prevent any digital encroachment across those boundaries. Those who divide their time in this way find their effectiveness in both of these areas improves.

In many ways, the principle of authenticity means applying the principles of focus and concentration in all situations at all times.

Explanation of the Problem

Lack of authenticity is an insidious problem in the modern workplace. Businesspeople spend significantly too much time with digital distractions such as frittering significant amounts of time with social media, electronic devices, gabbing on the cell phone, and texting endlessly about trivial items. According to research presented at the American Psychological Association, these digital influences can have harmful effects among teens and young adults, including narcissism, poor mental health, and diminished school performance.[6]

The problem of distraction is a large one in our current culture. If not carefully monitored, technology can distract us from our core activities. It's easy to blur the lines between professional and personal activities on the Internet. According to the American Sociological Review based on a study of 1,800 workers, nearly half of American workers bring work home with them regularly.[7] The temptation for these persons is that they start out working and end up surfing the Internet for a new cell phone or other gadget. Some of these workers may be parents of young children, and "The Wall Street Journal reports that a growing number of child-health experts and law-enforcement officials believe the increase in injuries [for young children] since 2007 may be due in part to parents who are distracted by mobile devices like smartphones.[8]

---

[6] "Social Networking's Good and Bad Impacts on Kids," *American Psychological Association Press Releases*. American Psychological Association, 6 Aug. 2011. Web. 5 Jul. 2011.

[7] Sharon Jayson, "Working at Home: Family-friendly?" *USA Today*, Gannett, 16 Apr. 2010. Web, 10 Apr. 2011.

[8] Worthen, Ben, "Injury Rate for Young Kids Increased Again Last Year," *The Wall Street Journal*. Dow Jones, 11 Oct. 2012. Web, 11 Oct. 2012.

Here are some examples of this blurring of activities:
1. Your employer pays you to focus your mind on a particular objective, and then you may get distracted during a meeting because you're receiving some text from your husband.
2. Your daughter wants you to attend her soccer game, and you review some spreadsheets from work during the game.
3. You kneel down to pray and hear the background noise of the television or radio.
4. You take a walk in the woods to resolve a pressing issue and you end up taking a phone call from a friend.
5. You, your wife, and your troubled teen are talking about a challenging issue, and you just can't keep yourself from checking the score from a big football game.

Digital distractions are frequently self-centered either through personal gratification, feeding one's ego by connecting with so many people in social media circles, or filling one's mind with trivial information (Internet surfing). Frequently, these distractions are ego driven, and they must be minimized.

When we are digitally distracted, not only do we get our priorities mixed up but we also are not faithful to our commitments. Working at work and playing at play is both the *right* choice and the *ethical* choice. Many businesspeople damage their relationships by their digital distractions.

By knowing your vision for an activity, planning carefully, avoiding traps found in use of media, and wisely apportioning your time, you will be better prepared to live a life of integrity and have successful purposes both in your work and in your personal/family affairs.

Self-Evaluation

Once again, you may not have a problem with this principle or you may be challenged by only one aspect of this general issue. To evaluate yourself, ask yourself how often you perform the following tasks. 1=never, 2=infrequently, 3=sometimes, 4=often, 5=always. Then proceed to the next section to learn how you can better perform a particular task.

	1	2	3	4	5
1. I am decisive about how I leverage my time.					
2. I recognize the disruptiveness of digital distractions.					
3. From time to time I take a digital vacation.					
4. I track my digital activities.					
5. I exercise caution when working with digital media when I am tired.					
6. I note and avoid digital selfishness.					

Solutions

For you to overcome these issues, I recommend the following six-point plan.

1. Make a decision about how you want to leverage your time

You have a choice to waste your time by building up your ego with trivial media interactions or to **leverage** your time by maximizing your impact with your relationships, your work, and your personal development. The overarching principle is being true to your values, goals, and relationships. When one uses time wisely (and uses media wisely), one has integrity. Integrity is a system of living one's life with purpose and meaningfulness so as to achieve excellence in all that one does.

AUTHENTICITY

Janet

Janet is an excellent real estate agent. She sets aside certain times for her prospecting time and then returns calls, checks email, and is responsive during the afternoon. She is a highly focused person. She is very responsive to people because she lets them know when she is available. She has integrity to herself by making important marketing calls, she has authenticity with her clients by communicating expectations to them, and she is responsible to her employer by fulfilling her agent responsibilities.

2. Believe that digital distractions are a distraction

Although businesspeople frequently benefit from the use of digital tools, if they are to become fully successful they need to come to a near-religious belief that most **digital distractions** are not actually work. While it's possible to get business from social media or it's nice to learn items on the Internet, in most cases it's simply a pleasant diversion from actual work. I encourage you, then, to see a digital distraction as a reward or break after completing a strategic item.

My son emailed his teacher one Saturday with a question about a homework assignment. The teacher was just five minutes away from walking down the aisle for his wedding, and my son's email triggered his smartphone--which the teacher noticed was on. Obviously, that teacher needed to prepare by turning off his digital distraction—his smartphone—prior to his wedding.

3. Take a digital vacation

To kick-start your new discipline, go on a **one-week media vacation** to get some of the media addictiveness out of your system. I have used this practice many times. It's incredibly painful at first; but then as it goes on, it feels really good. I have found that an occasional digital vacation helps me be happier, have more time, and feel like I have more control in my life.

David

Recently, I took a vacation to Switzerland and told clients, friends, and family that I wouldn't check voicemail, email, or texts during the entire trip. And I didn't. I was totally focused on my wife, my family, and the Swiss Alps. To call the vacation therapeutic is an understatement. It was an opportunity to become totally detached from the problems I was facing in the United States. In Switzerland, I was completely free to just relax and enjoy the mountain air. Because of this relaxation, I was able to focus better and work harder once I got back to the U.S. It's no wonder that after I got back, I was able to close many big deals and move the business forward in a powerful way.

4. Track your digital activities

Use of a time log for just a few days can be incredibly helpful because you become **aware** of the real use of your time. Frequently, the time spent involved with Internet news, Facebook, IM, or other small distractions seems so small that psychologically these minutes "shouldn't count." It's similar to the person trying to lose weight saying that "jelly beans at the secretary's desk don't count because they're so small." Short stints of time do count, and they do add up. The best way to recognize the real cost is to perform an occasional time log. Frequently, digital distractions are often acts of denial. Because we don't think that they actually cost time, they're somehow considered "free time." However, wasteful activities take persons away from the work they have and the relationships they want.

Some strategies you can take to enhance your power are these:

- **Minimizing.** One strategy many health-conscious professionals recognize is that by minimizing the amount of time that they spend on Facebook, social media, texting, cell phones, email, television, video games, etc., they are able to maximize the full use of their body and promote greater health. There is a strong link between higher use of digital distractions and poor health. Columbia Business School conducted a study and found that "people who spent more time online and who had a high percentage of close ties in their [social media] network were more likely to engage in binge eating and to have a greater body mass index."[9]

- **Review.** A very difficult activity for some professionals is to have a friend occasionally review the quantity of their text messages. This is an exceptionally painful activity because professionals quickly find out how much trivia they're engaged in. Just knowing that your friend will review these messages occasionally will have a positive impact on the volume of your texting.
- **Tracking of time.** Tracking time spent with digital devices is especially helpful because it gives the professional some accountability. Most professionals have no idea how much time they're actually spending on the Internet, in texting, on cell phones, etc. After the professional has started to track time, then he or she can set goals to use the time most effectively. The real benefit comes when a friend or mentor gauges whether the quantity is just right or too much.
- **Goal setting.** After tracking the time, you can set a goal for a reasonable amount of time with digital devices.
- **Pay to play.** Pay for all of your texts or extended calls. By doing this, you come to understand that nothing is free. You learn that your waste of time

---

[9] Bernstein, Elizabeth, "Why We Are So Rude Online," *The Wall Street Journal*. Dow Jones, 1 Oct. 2012. Web, 1 Oct. 2012.

on a meaningless phone call or with a useless text actually costs you money.
- **Filters.** Set up filters (both sites and times) at work to keep employees (including yourself) from frittering away time on pornography, gambling, Facebook, YouTube, and other time-consuming websites. Also, have the courage to review websites regularly with your employees. If they know that you'll talk with them about all of the sites that they visit, they'll likely act responsibly.

5. Exercise caution when working with digital media when you are tired

Digital distractions often occur when businesspeople are tired. Smart professionals thus avoid media use when they're tired, knowing they'll have a harder time breaking away when they're not at their best. Digital distractions are inherently easy, so they need to be completely avoided when one is tired. It's really important to use the media when you are feeling strong so that you can stay in control of your use and not let it control you. Become aware of the addictiveness of the Internet and all things digital. We may think that we're stronger than the Internet, but clever marketers make social media and websites so interesting that it's hard to get off those sites. By being aware of the addictiveness of the Internet, you have a better chance of keeping your balance.

6. Recognize digital selfishness

It's critical to recognize the fallacy that your social media friends are as important as your real friends. Unfortunately, people often gain more appreciation, interest, and self-gratification from their friends on the Internet than they get from the people in front of them (supervisor, co-workers, family, etc.). However, by recognizing and avoiding the trap of digital distraction, you unleash your ability to have true friendships.

Acknowledgements

In addition to our wives, to whom this book is dedicated, we wish to thank several others whose help was vital in completing this project: Beverly Snow who provided superb editorial and personal help; Culler Stuart who believed in us and gave us enough belief in ourselves to complete such an effort; James Gough who gave creative support; and all the clients at Coaching Solutions, LLC, and Audio Group, LLC who love reading and learning and care so much about personal development. They are the real teachers in this book.

We also wish to thank all of our many readers, who were kind enough to review early drafts of this book and offered helpful suggestions as to how to improve it: Brad Ayers, Michelle B., Rebecca Bar-Shain, Loree Connors, CJ Durachinsky, Nancy Emerman, Richard Fox, Jeff Hexter, Tracy Knuff, Kelcey Lehrich, Jim Levine, Kip Marlow, Keith Martinet, Sarah Minneman, Dick Myers, Brighton Rust, Mark Rust, Michael Rust, Patricia Rust, Richard Rust, Valentina Shimizu, Culler Stuart, Del Tanner, Bob Vecchio, and Pamela Winters.

About the Authors

David B. Rust is a business coach and owner of Coaching Solutions, LLC. With over twenty years of diverse corporate and entrepreneurial experience in the private and public sector plus an MBA from the University of North Carolina at Chapel Hill, David applies practical experience to help his clients achieve more from life and business. While working with business leaders over the last eleven years, he noticed that many had a growing problem with digital distraction. Because of this common issue, David decided to write a book that shares some of the counsel he has given to and learned from his clients.

Bradley J. Kramer is an accomplished writer with extensive experience in business, technical, scholarly, and creative writing. Brad oscillates between three geographical areas that form the "Bermuda Triangle" of his life: Cincinnati, where he grew up and worked for a number of years; Provo, Utah, where he attended college and wrote for a small computer company; and Chapel Hill, North Carolina, where, he did graduate work in English, was employed by a large computer company. Brad also enjoys tennis, which he plays almost daily.

www.ingramcontent.com/pod-product-compliance
Lightning Source LLC
Chambersburg PA
CBHW051634170526
45167CB00001B/183